Why A Christian Can And Should Vote For A Mormon in 2012

JAMES A. HALE

DEDICATION

To my wife Cindy who loves our Lord and has been my copy editor for the last 5 years and has helped me raise three lovely ladies, Candace, Ashley and Reagan and to my earthly father Frank Hale who knew something about the Cultural Mandate as well as the Evangelistic Mandate of believers.

CONTENTS

INTRODUCTION

Since the time of Christ, no society has ever been fully "Christian." Believers and unbelievers have always lived within the same society. However, few would deny that every place that the church of Jesus Christ has had a cultural effect radical change soon followed.

As voters in the United States align on political fronts and ready themselves for the upcoming 2012 election, they both look to defend their cause and dismantle the other side's agenda. The same should hold true with the Christian Church and its voters

Key issues this year stem from the very questionable agenda of President Obama. One concern rests in the growing authority of the Federal government over its individual citizens. This causes many to wonder just how close Communism is to taking over the realm of power in the United States. This is an issue for Christians because Communism is an Atheist based government.

Moral issues will again play a key role for Christians in the election. President Obama has made moral issues even bigger by siding with efforts to advance homosexual life styles and attack the innocent unborn child. These are two issues that the Christian church by far oppose.

Now these moral issues have been in past elections, but there is a new issue that the church must look at this year. That is, can a Christian really vote for a Mormon? Is political support for someone outside the Christian faith allowed in Scripture? If you vote for a Mormon, is this in turn giving support for Mormonism?

If a Mormon wins the election does this mean that Mormonism will be the national religion?

The answer for the Mormon issues will be dealt with lastly in this book, after we establish the churches role in the state and the main issues to consider this election. If you bought this book only for this reason, simply skip to the chapter "Why a Christian can and should vote for a Mormon in 2012" and read it. However, let me encourage you go back later and read the whole book as I build a case for the church's active role in our government.

THE OLD STATE VS CHURCH ISSUE

In this election Christian believers ask themselves old questions about the church and its role with the state. What are we to say about faith and politics? Does not the Bible tell us to stay away from politics, because it is God that places leaders in office? Can we as a church have a voice in the government? And how about our nation's laws? Does not the law forbid churches from getting into politics?   Should government even matter to the church?

This book will answer emphatically, yes it does matter, and yes our nation's laws do allow the churches voice, and yes God's word does tell us that we should help shape our government. In answering these questions this book will look at church history, world history, our nation's history and Scripture. We will also review this nation's laws, as well as the law of God, which we call the Bible. We will also research theologians of the past to find what they say about our role in government.

From a theology standpoint I am Reformed. That is to say, my theology comes from the Protestant reformation. Therefore the theologians that I will quote will mainly come from the Reformed tradition. Reformed Systematic Theology books cover most all doctrine that surround the Christian faith.

YOU CAN'T LEGISLATE MORALITY

The often heard, "You can't legislate morality," has no good grounding in history. In fact, morality is the only foundation for law. Legislating morality does work and is good for society. Most people do not kill other humans because killing is morally wrong. "No speeding" signs do slow down most would be speeders. Even abortion (a subject where "you can't legislate morality" is used) was limited before it was legalized and we had fewer abortions then than today.

Didn't some still have abortions when there were laws against it? Yes, and some still speed in their cars, some still steal from banks, and some still lie on the witness stand even with laws that say this is wrong. We will always have law breakers. However, laws limit immoral behavior because morality is legislated now and it works.

WHY THIS BOOK?

Over the last few years I have seen Christian's tongue tied, not knowing how to answer post-modern thought in politics. Most of these answers they do know but do not feel at liberty to give an answer within our culture, because of fear of offending people. This fear is wrongly felt because Christians can be bold about the truth of Scripture.

After over 200 years of freedom to worship as we feel convicted, I once believed that most Christians took for granted that they could go to the church of their choice. They took for granted that they could express their views about God and still prosper within the society with only minor attacks from those that hate God.

Now I see us in a new era where most Christians are seeing the attacks on the church increasing especially in the last four years and they are not sure what to do about it. Sadly many of these attacks come from our leaders in Washington that seemed focused on destroying the Christian faith. Christians see these attacks and are concerned that their freedoms are in danger of being taken from them. The freedom to worship our God as we please is not assured by any one anymore.

What are we to do? Prayer is a given action we must take, but are there also things that we can do as voters in this nation? Are there things that we can say as pastors to help lead the church in voting issues?

It is my desire that this book will show that the church does have a voice in civil government, but should use that voice now before they lose it to those that hate God.

I do love this nation, but I have a greater love for my God. I do hope that the Church of Jesus Christ will let it's voice be known in this election and turn back the forces that seek to destroy us.

PART 1
A godly society

1) WHY WORK TOWARD A GODLY SOCIETY?

Theologian Louis Berkhof who first published his work in the 1930's has a rather large section on the church. Berkhof agrees with the early Reformers, that the church is both visible and invisible. The invisible church is all the body of the elect who are known only to God. The visible church becomes visible when the church gathers to worship God. This is referred to by some as the local church.

The Christian church has always held that the visible church is made up of believers and non-believers and that God is the only one that knows who is his sheep in the fold.

The invisible church has but one Shepherd, Christ. The visible church has under-shepherds (pastors/elders) to lead the flock.

> Acts 20: 28
> Pay careful attention to yourselves and to all the flock, in which the Holy Spirit has made you overseers, to care for the church of God, which he obtained with his own blood.

Please notice in Berkhof's following quote about the two natures of the visible church. In terms that seem perhaps too military to us, the church is described as the "church militant," or those that were living, still deeply engaged in the great cosmic spiritual battle. Those who are dead in Christ are the "church triumphant," now reigning with Christ.

BERKHOF ON THE MILITANT CHURCH

> "The church in the present dispensation is a militant Church, that is, she is called unto, and is actually engaged in, a holy warfare. This, of course, does not mean that she must spend her strength in self-destroying internecine struggles, but that she is duty bound to carry on an incessant warfare against the hostile world in every form in which it reveals itself, whether in the church or outside of it, and against all spiritual forces of darkness. The church may not spend all her time in prayer and meditation, however necessary and important these may be, nor may she rest on her oars in the peaceful enjoyment of her Lord, fighting in a war that is both offensive and defensive."

A militant church conjures up many images. Some of those images, we may not like to think of the church in that way. But one thing is for sure. Berkhof does not use words that paint pacifism. Is Berkhof's image a fitting example of what Christ desired for his church? Can such an image be supported with Scripture?

Since God is in control, and since we all believe it is His power that builds the church, are we even to be aggressive in efforts to expand the church, or simply be passive and watch God work? Is the growth of the church only measured in the numbers in the church? In other words, do we have other mandates, other than sharing the gospel, that God has laid on the church, in order to accomplish His will?

If aggressiveness is allowed, how far do we take it? Does this Militant church reach into all areas of life? Do we battle the evil forces at work, school and within the government, or are we to just view them as the kingdom of the world and something that God never intended on changing because of His new Kingdom he is building?

THE CHURCH'S VIEW OF THE LAW OF GOD

We begin by looking at the church's position of God's Law. There is a three fold purpose of God's law in the Protestant faith. John Calvin, for example, wrote of the Law:

The first purpose of the law is to be a mirror. On the one hand, the law of God reflects and mirrors the perfect righteousness of God. The law tells us much about who God is. Perhaps more important, the law illumines human sinfulness. Augustine wrote, "The law orders, that we, after attempting to do what is ordered, and so feeling our weakness under the law, may learn to implore the help of grace." The law highlights our weakness so that we might seek the strength found in Christ. Here the law acts as a severe schoolmaster who drives us to Christ.

A second purpose for the law is the restraint of evil. The law, alone, cannot change human hearts. It can, however, serve to protect the righteous from the unjust. Calvin says this purpose is "by means of its fearful denunciations and the consequent dread of punishment, to curb those who, unless forced, have no regard for rectitude and justice." The law allows for a limited measure of justice on this earth, until the last judgment is realized.

The third purpose of the law is to reveal what is pleasing to God. As born-again children of God, the law enlightens us as to what is pleasing to our Father, whom we seek to serve. The Christian delights in the law as God Himself delights in it. Jesus said, "If you love Me, keep My commandments" (John 14:15). This is the highest function of the law, to serve as an instrument for the people of God to give Him honor and glory.

It is within the second purpose of the law "restraint of evil," where I will build my first argument.

> *1 Timothy 2:2*
> *(PRAY) for kings and all who are in high positions, that we may lead a peaceful and quiet life, godly and dignified in every way.*

Good government helps people to live a peaceful and godly life and bad government hinders that. 1 Timothy 2 says we should pray for this peaceful life. Verse 3 says that this praying for a peaceful and quiet life is "good" and that it "pleases God, our Savior."

The peaceful life for the church, leading to a healthy church, is seen many times throughout the ages. Some may ask,"But isn't the church stronger when it suffers? When the church has it "good," corruption enters into the ranks." The corruption that many see in a moderately suffering church period does indeed come about, but only after a generation or two after the church has left an oppressive time. However, before this corruption comes, we often see the greatest growth in the church. A look into church history verifies this claim.

IMPERIAL CHURCH HISTORY

Many place the Imperial church under Constantine and the Holy Roman Empire in the same camp. This would however be wrong to do so. The Holy Roman Empire was a failed effort by man to pull the great Roman Empire back together. The Imperial church on the other hand was a heathy government, led by Constantine who worshiped the "Sun god," even though he said he was a believer in Christ. He may have become a true believer later on, but clearly even after he saw his vision, he remained pagan.

Before Constantine, the church lived through great and horrific persecution. Early Christians were persecuted, at the hands of both Jews and the Roman Empire which controlled much of the land that early Christianity was distributed across. This continued from the first century until the early fourth century when Christianity was legalized by Constantine.

What happened during the time of the Imperial church? It was during this time, that of the council of Nicea, Athanasius writers, Basil the Great, and the Council of Constantinople produced great writings. We also have the great works of Jerome and Augustine from this time.

The Roman Empire was Christian in name only but this had stopped years of great persecution in the church. Clearly this was a good time for the church. The leaders were at "peace" (1 Tim 2) to set doctrine and write their works. It was a Political Christian, Constantine, the head of state, that called for council of Nicea.

Political Christianity is not to be viewed as the same as the church. Political Christians may or may not be true believers. Political Christianity views the Christian faith in good light and this helps bring about laws that make the church's ministry "peaceable." The church was at peace with the government in Constantine's day, because God had providentially ordained the government head (Constantine) to pass laws that allowed the church to express their faith openly. This can be seen over and over in church history.

ENGLAND 1500-1700

English Bible translator, William Tyndale, while being executed cried out..."*LORD OPEN THE KING OF ENGLAND'S EYES.*"

Henry VIII was the King of England, and never became a believer as far as we know. He was the king that murdered his wives if he didn't like them. Yet he did become a Political Christian if only for selfish reasons. God can and does use the sins of man to bring about his will.

In 1532, Thomas Cranmer was appointed the resident ambassador at the court of the Holy Roman Emperor, Charles V. As Charles traveled, Cranmer went with him and while passing through the Lutheran city of Nuremberg, Cranmer was able to see for the first time the effects of the Reformation.

At some point, Cranmer become Reformed in his theology. Cranmer also fell in love with a Lutheran woman while in Germany, and married her. This was forbidden in the church, so he had his wife hidden in a box while they traveled.

It is certain that Cranmer's wife who was a Lutheran, had an impact on her husband, who would soon be the Archbishop. As Archbishop, Cranmer helped push for the Thirty-Nine Articles. The Thirty-Nine Articles of Religion were established in 1563 and are the Anglican doctrine in relation to the controversies of the English Reformation; especially in relation to Calvinist doctrine. Mrs. Cranmer didn't keep her faith hidden from the soon to be ruling Archbishop, but rather influenced the church leader with her faith.

Later that year (1532), was when King Henry appointed Thomas Cranmer, the Archbishop of Canterbury. Henry did this only to help himself secure the marriage of his new wife.

Cranmer and his wife influenced Henry in appointing Thomas Cromwell as the "chief minister" to the King. Cromwell was a key evangelical figure. All of this time the King remained a non-believer, but the church helped shape his Political Christian stance. Now it is certain that the Cranmers and Cromwell would have loved to have seen Henry become a believer, but they did not let his unbelief stop them from doing what would be good for the church as well as society.

Then you have Anne Boleyn. King Henry the VIII married Anne who was an active sponsor of evangelicalism and who imported and distributed large quantities of evangelical literature. Anne introduced the King personally to Reformed theology. This led to the opening of the door to the Protestant Reformation.

It is unmistakable that Henry only used the Protestant Reformation in a political move to gain more control from the Pope. Henry never formally repudiated the doctrines of the Roman Catholic Church, but he declared himself supreme head of the church in England. However, please note that the new Political Christian position that Henry had taken, restrained the evil and oppression in which the Protestant believers found themselves and helped the church spread the gospel.

Anne was wrongly investigated for high treason, arrested and beheaded. This, too, helped the Reformation. Anne became a key figure not only in the religious upheaval, but also in the political upheaval that was the start of the English Reformation. As stated before, it is important to remember that some of those that pushed for the Protestant Reformation were not believers, but were using the Reformation for their own political gain and were therefore only Political Christians.

If we are honest, believers are fully aware that some politicians only hold up a Bible and quote a verse to get elected. They do this only to obtain the church's vote. Why would the church not support this, even if the politcians are not true believers, if indeed we feel they would pass laws that favor Christians? Is this not bringing the peace, or retaining the peace that allows us to worship?

Are we to think that God wants us to pray for peaceable times that allow for the spreading of the gospel and pray for rulers/kings and those who are in high positions that stand in favor of Christian values, yet not vocally support them from the pulpit when God has answered our prayer with such a leader? Surely this is twisted thinking and even a rejection of what God commands us from Scripture.

> *Philippians 4*
> *Finally, brothers, whatever is true, whatever is honorable, whatever is just, whatever is pure, whatever is lovely, whatever is commendable, if there is any excellence, if there is anything worthy of praise, think about these things.*

Notice "worthy of praise." If we are called to think of things that are worthy of praise, then those things which are indeed worthy of our praise, we must praise.

If we are to pray for leaders to bring or retain a nation that gives the church a peaceable environment which is used to spread the gospel, and if God answers our prayers, we are commanded by Scripture to sing praises to God, and praise the one God sent who is also worthy of that praise. In this case it would be the ruler God sent.

Let's say that we feel led to pray for a leader that does not support the aborting of babies. Let's also say that a leader arises that is an answer to that prayer. Are we to think that this is not to be praised? Surely we must agree that we are commanded to give praise, not only to God for his answer to prayer, but also to the man as a form of encouragement and influence. This we should do, even if he is not a believer. Of course we should also pray that he or she will someday believe in Christ and not just support the good found in Christianity.

The point is that Constantine, a Political Christian, was used by the early church. Anne Boleyn, Thomas Cranmer and his wife used Henry VIII, a murdering, non-believing   Political Christian, to bring about change that would restrain evil and help the church spread the gospel. The change came not from the church, but as the church influenced the government. When the government changed, God sent Queen Elizabeth who was not only a true believer, but the top government leader that passed laws allowing the Reformation to take hold in England.

Why would some say we should not be a strong influence in our government today? Surely to affirm this would be foolish.

2) REVOLUTION IN ENGLAND AND THE UNITED STATES

In chapter one we looked at Constantine's time. Raymond Van Dam wrote a book called "The Roman Revolution of Constantine." In it Van Dam says that Constantine's patronage of Christianity required both a new theology of the Christian Trinity and a new political image of a Political Christian emperor. We have shown this to be true.

We have also considered whether the church has a mandate in Scripture to work toward a godly society on earth, or is the church just simply to wait for our new earth. Thus far, we have examined only a few verses for governing principals that believers are to apply to their lives and looked more into church history to see how the church of the past has applied these principals to the government that they live under.

The main principal is that we are to pray for a good government that is at peace with the church, and praise those that God sends to give us good government, because good government is good for the church and good for all mankind.

Christian's often do not think of how the church has obtained freedom to preach and share the gospel. They look at triumphant times of the church and rejoice in them, but forget that a revolution with men fighting with guns and swords took place to bring those freedoms to us. This is not limited to the American Revolution although it certainly includes the American Revolution. A Revolution took place just before nearly all the times of a healthy church environment period.

REVOLUTION IN ENGLAND AND THE UNITED STATES

In England there came the so-called Glorious Revolution of William and Mary that led to the English Bill of Rights. A year after the Glorious Revolution, the Act of Toleration law was put in place on May 24, 1689. This allowed the London Baptist Confession to come out of the closet and be openly proclaimed.

One reason why the London Baptist Confession was written was because the Anglican church abandoned the Westminster Confession which led to an English Baptist persecution. In 1677 a group met and wrote a Baptist Confession very close to the Westminster Confession. This was all done underground and never endorsed because of persecution. Baptist preacher John Bunyan was one that was in and out of jail in the 1660s and 1670s because of this persecution.

Did the church pass laws to bring peace on the church? No, it was the government that passed the Act of Toleration law and not the church. This restrained evil allowing the Baptist faith to be proclaimed and preached by men who came after Bunyan.

WHY DID WILLIAM AND MARY
PASS THE TOLERANCE ACT?

Prince William Henry, the William of the William and Mary domain, was born in 1650, was raised by his mother until he entered the University of Leiden. He was raised by his mother to be a Reformed believer. In 1688, Prince William accepted an invitation by a small Protestant group to become King of England. He defeated the regular parliamentarian army, conquered London and became king.

I have no idea if William was a true believer or not. If he indeed was a true believer, you may think that this is no way for a believer to act.

Writer John MacArthur, whom I highly admire, makes this point regarding America's fore-fathers, by saying,

> " the United States was actually born out of a violation of the New Testament principles, and any blessings that God has bestowed on America have come in spite of that disobedience by the Founding Fathers"
> **(From: Why Government Can't save You)**

MacArthur also says,

> "Jesus did not come to earth to make the old creation moral through social and governmental reform but to make a new creatures(His people) holy through the saving power of the gospel and transforming work of the Holy Spirit."

While I agree with MacArthur that the end goal is to make new creatures, I disagree that we are not to reform all of life. This philosophy of the church in our culture expressed by MacArthur is nothing new. This is the same philosophy expressed by other great men of the past.

Another Reformed teacher that I greatly admire holds to this school of thought.

Dr. Martyn Lloyd-Jones who is a theological hero of mine, said this in his great book "Studies in the Sermon on the Mount," in the chapter "The salt of the earth":

> *"There are those who say that the Christian should act as salt of the earth meaning the church makes pronouncement about the general situation of the world, about political, economic and international affairs and other such subjects. Undoubtedly in many churches, if not in the vast majority, that in how this text would be interpreted. People denounce communism, and talk about war, the international situation, and other similar problems. They say that the Christian functions as salt of the earth in this general way, by making these comments about the world situation. Now, as I see it, this is a most serious misunderstanding of scriptural teaching."*
> **(Martyn Lloyd-Jones - Studies in the Sermon on the Mount,/The salt of the earth)**

While I love these men greatly and thank God for raising them up to lead our church, I must also disagree with them in this area. The few examples given so far, have shown that this influencing of the culture and government leaders, is indeed part of church history that proceeded a blessed time in the church. There are many more examples to pull from.

The point to see here is not if William should have invaded England, but that the believers (the church) asked him to invade. But I suppose it is fair to ask, and indeed we can learn some things if we do ask, why did William invade?

William of (William and Mary) was driven in some ways by his view of God as he was taught by his mother. This caused William to answer the call from believers and dare I say the call of God, as God worked in the hearts of believers, to be King of England and to enact Laws that would help the church.

What shall we say of those Protestants that asked William to invade? Well, we cannot blame them for doing nothing, which I'm sorry to say is what many Christians believe we should do today. The Christians of that day didn't just sit around hoping that God would send a King to free them. I'm sure that they prayed to this end. I'm also sure they placed their trust in God to answer their prayer. It is also clear they saw William as a God-sent answer to their prayer. They acted on what they saw in the character of a man in power, then reached out, asking William to become King and set them free.

I'm fairly sure the church of that day felt William, if King, would help pass laws that would restrain evil and help the church spread the gospel. History tells us this is what happened.

PURITAN MOVEMENT AND AMERICA

The churches influence in England is the same influence in government found in the heart of the Puritans whom help found this nation. It would not be right to say that this nation had all Christian leaders, for clearly this was not the case. But it is very clear that the Church influenced the government's lawmaking.

The Mayflower Compact, the first governing document of Plymouth Colony states:

> *"Having undertaken, for the Glory of God and advancement of the Christian Faith and Honour of our King and Country, a Voyage to plant the First Colony in the Northern Parts of Virginia, do by these presents solemnly and mutually in the presence of God and one of another, Covenant and Combine ourselves together into a Civil Body Politic, for our better ordering and preservation and furtherance of the ends aforesaid; and by virtue hereof to enact, constitute and frame such just and equal Laws, Ordinances, Acts, Constitutions and Offices, from time to time, as shall be thought most meet and convenient for the general good of the Colony, unto which we promise all due submission and obedience."*

The Pilgrims and the Puritans, two important early groups of settlers, were Christian. The Reformed, Presbyterian and Congregationalist churches, all had significant colonial denominations at the time of the American Revolution. These Christians didn't just study Scripture, but desired governments that would allow them to worship God. They didn't just pray to this end, but worked towards that end.

Take the United States Declaration of Independence. It begins with *"endowed by their Creator with certain unalienable Rights"* and ends with, *"with a firm reliance on the protection of Divine Providence."*

God rejecting men did not come up with these words on their own. I admit that such wording is not indicative of a Christian author, but it does show there must have been a believer's influence on the authors for them to have written those words. This alone suggests that the church made a Godly impact on the new government.

Still, one cannot deny that virtually all of these signers and original congressmen and senators were Christians and identified as members of specific denominations, such as Episcopalian, Presbyterian, Congregationalist, etc. Is one to think that these men of faith said nothing of their faith while they were leaders? Surely one must conclude that the words found in many documents of this nation, came about from the believer's influence either directly or indirectly on those writing these documents.

Many of these men were not just believers, but were Reformed believers. Of the 165 different men who were signers of Declaration of Independence, signers of the U.S. Constitution, or who were Senators or Representatives in the First Federal Congress, 21 were Congregationalists, 20 were Presbyterians, 5 were Dutch Reformed or German Reformed and one was a Huguenot. Of these individuals whose denominations were officially Reformed denominations, we can say that at least 48 or (29%) of the founding fathers were Reformed believers.

WE HAVE A CALL FROM SCRIPTURE TO MAKE A DIFFERENCE IN THE WORLD

These early leaders of our nation understood what it meant to be the "salt of the earth" as I feel as it is meant to be understood. The *"salt of the earth"* comes from the same passage where we are told that we are a "City on a Hill."

> Matthew 5..
> *"You are the salt of the earth, but if salt has lost its taste, how shall its saltiness be restored? It is no longer good for anything except to be thrown out and trampled under people's feet. "You are the light of the world. A city set on a hill cannot be hidden."*

This meaning held by the Reformed believers that founded this nation is also found in many if not most Reformed theology writings.

Cambridge Commentary,

Salt is essential to all organized life, it is also the great preservative from corruption. If these virtues pass from it, it is worse than useless. It cannot even be thrown on the fields, it must be cast into the street to be trodden under foot.

Jamieson, Fausset & Brown,

In Scripture, mankind, under the unrestrained workings of their own evil nature, are represented as entirely corrupt. Thus, before the flood (Ge 6:11, 12); after the flood (Ge 8:21); in the days of David (Ps 14:2, 3); in the days of Isaiah (Isa 1:5, 6); and in the days of Paul (Eph 2:1-3; see also Job 14:4; 15:15, 16; Joh 3:6; compared with Ro 8:8; Tit 3:2, 3). The remedy for this, says our Lord, is the active presence of His disciples among their fellows.

The character and principles of Christians, brought into close contact with it, are designed to arrest the festering corruption of humanity and season it's insipidity. But how, it may be asked, are Christians to do this office for their fellow men, if their righteousness only exasperate them, and recoil, in every form of persecution, upon themselves? The answer is: That is but the first and partial effect of their Christianity upon the world: though the great proportion would dislike and reject the truth, a small but noble band would receive and hold it fast; and in the struggle that would ensue, one and another even of the opposing party would come over to His ranks, and at length the Gospel would carry all before it.

Barnes' Notes,

Salt renders food pleasant and palatable, and preserves from putrefaction. So Christians, by their lives and instructions, are to keep the world from entire moral corruption. By bringing down, by their prayers, the blessing of God, and by their influence and example, they save the world from universal vice and crime.

Dr E. Hastings,

Salt keeps things from going bad..... The Good man, as Jesus conceived him, is a kind of moral antiseptic in human society.......It (salt) eats into the roots of moral corruption. It quickens conscience. It awakens shame.

William Hendriksen,

...the potency of salt as an antiseptic, a substance that prevents and retards decay, upon which the emphasis falls here.....It combats deterioration. Similarly Christians, by showing themselves to be Christians indeed, are constantly combating moral and spiritual decay.

William Barclay,

It (salt in the ancient world) was used to keep things from going bad and rotten, and to hold decay and putrefaction at bay....salt preserves from corruption. If a Christian is to be salt of the earth, he must have a certain antiseptic influence on life.

James Montgomery Boice,

According to Jesus, the Christian is clearly to influence his society. And this must be true wherever the principles of the gospel impinge upon the religious, political, economic, or social issues of the Christian Community.

* Now you may not have read all the men just quoted, but please take the time to read these quotes by the next two men.

John MacArthur

So our Lord is saying that since we have a decaying, corrupted society shrouded in darkness, this society needs salt to retard the corruption and light to brighten the darkness.

Martyn Lloyd-Jones on the same passage:

The principal function of salt is to preserve and act as an antiseptic.....(salt) is more negative rather than positive. I wonder how often we conceive of ourselves in this way, as agents in the world meant to prevent this particular process of putrefaction and decay?

These last two quotes beg to ask this question:
How does MacArthur and others make statements like this one from Lloyd-Jones?

"The moment the Church begins to intervene in these political, social and economic matters, she is hampering and hindering herself in her God-appointed task of evangelism. She can no longer say that she 'knows no man after the flesh' and thereby she is sinning. Let the individual play his part as a citizen, and belong to any political party that he may choose. ...The Church is not concerned as a church about these things."?

HOW DOES LLOYD-JONES JUSTIFY HIS STANCE?

Dr. Lloyd-Jones tries to make a distinction between the church and the individual believer in this area. Lloyd-Jones supports this distinction with an example of history of his own, using William Wilberforce as a model to follow. Wilberforce fought for years to abolish slavery in the United Kingdom.

I cannot follow this line of thinking by Lloyd-Jones for two main reasons. The first reason is that this is contrary to Scripture.

Romans 12:4-5 says:
> "For as in one body we have many members, and the members do not all have the same function so we, though many, are one body in Christ, and individually members one of another"

Paul is telling us here that we are all to work together as one and not as separate individuals, but each of us have different functions. This same idea is brought up again in 1 Corinthians:

> For just as the body is one and has many members, and all the members of the body, though many, are one body, so it is with Christ. For in one Spirit we were all baptized into one body—Jews or Greeks, slaves or free—and all were made to drink of one Spirit.
> For the body does not consist of one member but of many. If the foot should say, "Because I am not a hand, I do not belong to the body," that would not make it any less a part of the body. And if the ear should say, "Because I am not an eye, I do not belong to the body," that would not make it any less a part of the body. If the whole body were an eye, where would be the sense of hearing? If the whole body were an ear, where would be the sense of smell? But as it is, God arranged the members in the body, each one of them, as he chose. If all were a

single member, where would the body be? As it is, there are many parts, yet one body.

Scripture demands us not to be a church that acts as bunch of renegades, but encourages us to work together as one.

We also must look at how others have applied this throughout the history of the church.

Dr. John Frame who is maybe the foremost American Christian philosopher said:

> *Now some have argued that cultural transformation is the work of Christian individuals, but not of the local church. They argue that the latter should be limited to the area of the "spiritual," the preaching of the gospel and the administration of the sacraments. But the spiritual/secular distinction is not biblical. The gospel as proclaimed by John (Matt. 3:2), Jesus (Matt. 4:17), Philip (Acts 8:12), and Paul (Acts 19:8, 20:25, 28:23, 28:31) announces the coming of the kingdom of God, a new order of righteousness, peace, and joy (Rom. 14:17). In the kingdom, we do all things (not just "spiritual") to the glory of God (1 Cor. 10:31), all things in the name of the Lord Jesus (Col. 3:17). It is plain that care for the poor, orphans, and widows is part of that. (published in Nine Marks Journal (Nov. - Dec., 2007))*
> **(John Frame On The Role Of The Local Church In Cultural Transformation)**

Being the salt of the earth is a commandment of Scripture and comes from our Lord himself. All Protestants, both then and now will agree that God's Holy Word is the final authority. The Roman church, says the church gave us Scripture, and therefore the church rests as high, or higher than Scripture. Therefore Rome places authority on early church fathers as well as Scripture.

The Reformers broke from Rome on the two fold authority of the believer and proclaimed Solo Scriptura. But the Reformers did not ignore the church fathers, but rather looked to them on how that they applied the truths that were found in Scripture. They used the church fathers to show that what the Reformers were writing, was not a new thought, but one that great men of the past had also found to be true.

Immediately we have a problem today following earlier Protestants in the area of civil government.

Never before the last 200 years, has such a government existed as we find in this nation. The early Protestants lived under an earthly king. The early church lived under an Emperor. The governments of the past were ran by a sovereign ruler of an empire or another type of imperial realm.

This is something that must be considered because of two reasons. First, there is a huge difference between the two forms of government. Under a King, there is sovereign rule decreed from one human. If the King says it's law, it is law. Second, those that want to limit the church's role in today's political economy, make the same economic distinction when it comes to the Old Testament and the New Testament.

Lloyd-Jones again from his book "Studies in the Sermon on the Mount"..

> "Ah, they say, but you get it in the prophets of the Old Testament. Yes; but the answer is that in the Old Testament the Church was the nation of Israel, and there was no distinction between Church and state. The prophets had therefore to address the whole nation and to speak about its entire life. But the new Testament is not identified with any nation or nations."
>
> **(Martyn Lloyd-Jones - Studies in the Sermon on the Mount)**

I do not agree with this statement because it falls short of what we see in Scripture.

Again John Frame from the same article says:

> "Is a failing school system, then, for example, the responsibility of the local church? Education is part of our kingdom responsibility (Deut. 6:6-9, Tit. 2:12), part of the gospel of the kingdom. This may mean encouraging believers to educate their children at home, or in Christian schools. It may mean advocating a new commitment to excellence in the public schools. It is better that schools not be administered directly by the church: that is not necessary and it can be a distraction. But where there is no alternative, yes, the church may start a school, bringing to its children (and even to children of non-Christian parents) the riches of human knowledge within a kingdom-centered worldview. There are legitimate questions as to how best to handle such matters in different localities. But the question is not, whether the

church has a responsibility, but how should it undertake that responsibility. The gospel of the kingdom is comprehensive—good news for every aspect of human life"

The gospel of the kingdom is indeed comprehensive.

HERE IS WHERE WE ARE TODAY

You may agree with John MacArthur, that the founders of this nation, should have never started the rebellion back in the 1700's, but there is no going back after 200 years. No one tells a new believer that has been divorced and remarried to correct that sin, by leaving his wife of today and heading back to his first wife. Likewise, if we believe this nation was born in sin, a position I will later debate, we don't sin again by overthrowing this government and handing it back to the King of England.

If you were born into this nation, it is God that has placed you here. This government, and not the old King of England, is the one you must deal with.

> *Titus 2:11-14*
> *For the grace of God has appeared, bringing salvation for all people, training us to renounce ungodliness and worldly passions, and to live self-controlled, upright, and godly lives in the present age, waiting for our blessed hope, the appearing of the glory of our great God and Savior Jesus Christ, who gave himself for us to redeem us from all lawlessness and to purify for himself a people for his own possession who are zealous for good works.*

3) WITHOUT A KING

The Bible commands all believers to honor their leaders and pray for them. 1 Timothy 2:1-4 says we should pray for our leaders. Now, it is a given that this prayer should include that God would grant our leaders wisdom in leading us. However, this is not the main reason we are to pray for them, going by the context of 1 Timothy 2. Mainly we are to pray that they will be saved from their sins, and thereby have the knowledge of the truth.

> *1 Tim 2*
> *(Pray) for kings and all who are in high positions, that we may lead a peaceful and quiet life, godly and dignified in every way. This is good, and it is pleasing in the sight of God our Savior, who desires all people to be saved and to come to the knowledge of the truth.*

What reasons does Paul give to us? Salvation of their souls is one. There is however another reason that Paul says we should pray for leaders. We are to pray for them, "that we may lead a peaceful and quiet life, godly and dignified in every way." The best way to have a peaceable government for the church, is to have our leaders become one of us. In other words, we should desire that they come to the truth of the gospel. This is best done when the believer not only prays for their leaders, but makes an effort to influence them.

All influence should be done with honor and respect. Some hold that this should only be done on an individual level as seen in chapter 2 of this study. This however goes against Scripture as we will see in chapter 5.

It was stated in chapter 2, that we must distinguish between our form of government and the king led monarch, when we look into history for reference. To distinguish between a monarchy and Imperial economy on one hand, and a Republic on the other hand, does not mean that the newer Republic state has no history to draw upon. We do have history, but it is limited to the last 200 years.

So we must ask; how have Christian men of the past 200 years, seen the nature of the church in this world? If aggressiveness is allowed, how far do we take it? Does the Militant church reach into all areas of life?

We start by going back to England where we first found this form of government. The British people no longer live under the direct hand of the King, but now have a parliamentary system. Parliamentary systems usually have a head of government and a head of state, with the head of government being the prime minister or premier, and the head of state often being a figurehead. Unlike the days of the King, the people of the land are allowed legal contribution into whom is the head of the government.

Charles Spurgeon, a hero of many Christians today, lived under a parliamentary system. But Spurgeon's admiration of today pales to his fame when he was alive. Spurgeon was even on the cover of Vanity Fair. As a national figure, Spurgeon's opinions were highly sought.

Spurgeon's opinions were asked on nearly every controversial subject. Spurgeon was asked if he was he opposed to pigeon shooting? What did he think about hooped skirts? Spurgeon was not quiet on these issues, but expressed his feelings about them to the media. He didn't say this is not the gospel, therefore I will not answer. He told them that he opposed both. If Charles Spurgeon made a statement about capital punishment, it was reported not only to the nation, but also world wide.

Charles Spurgeon wrote this letter:

> *To the Liberal Electors of Lambeth,*
> *Friends,*
> *I am informed by persons of judgement that if the Liberal cause should not succeed in Lambeth at this election, it can only be through the apathy of its professed supporters. I trust that no such apathy now exists, and that every Liberal elector will present himself at the poll. The crisis involves such weighty matters that every man should record his vote for that which he conscientiously believes to be the side of right. Indifference will be a crime against the best interest of the commonwealth.*

He ends his letter with this:

> *Imagine another six years of Tory rule, devoid alike of peace and progress, and you will rouse yourselves to do your duty, and all hazard of a repetition of the Southward disaster will be far away.*
> *Your friend and neighbor,*
> *C. H. Spurgeon*

In one sermon, Spurgeon ended it this way:

> *Southwark once led the van in advanced Liberalism, and it has now come down to be represented by two Conservatives! Will you not alter this state of things? Have you not had enough of it already? The remedy is in your own hands.*

How could Spurgeon say things like this with him knowing the Bible as well as he did? Had he not read Romans 13 ?

> *1Let every person be subject to the governing authorities. For there is no authority except from God, and those that exist have been instituted by God*

Again, I do not believe Spurgeon saw this passage as many do today in the United States. We will look at this passage later and see that Spurgeon was not going against the text. One thing is clear, Spurgeon saw liberty as God-given liberty, in the same light as the

God-given priesthood of the saint. The Reformers rejected the idea of the Roman church that teaches that there are high priests and that one must go through the high priest in order to confess sin. The Reformers upheld the priesthood of each believer, being able to go right to the throne of God in prayer. Like the priesthood of the saints, Spurgeon saw that the government that God had placed him under, was a government ran by the people and saw the governorship of all electors.

Therefore Spurgeon wrote:

> God has made us our own governors in these British Isles, for loyal as we are to our Queen, we practically are Caesars to ourselves.

I believe Spurgeon has this right. Romans 13 says we are to follow the rule of the governing authorities. In Spurgeon's case, this is not limited to a single human king/queen. Elected officials now lead the United Kingdom within the realms of the Parliamentary sovereignty. The highest British authority is no longer the king, but it is the Parliamentary sovereignty (also called parliamentary supremacy or legislative supremacy) with the King/Queen only as a figure head of the state. The statutes which govern England are laws passed by Parliament. Parliament law is England's supreme and final source.

It was political pressure from British Prime Minister Stanley Baldwin that caused Edward VIII, the then King of England, to abdicate from the throne in 1936. Two hundred years before, Baldwin would have been beheaded for treason. The Law of the land now prohibits this.

The highest person in government falls under the law of the land. A single human being no longer sets laws, but rather a group of laws written by many humans are enacted and carried over from one leader to the other. New leadership must follow the laws passed by the old leadership. This is done until many more humans get together and write new laws, vote on it and if they have enough votes, replace new laws overriding the old.

This is a citizen governorship in which God has placed the people of the United States. It's highest authority is not found in a human king, but found in written law.

THE GREAT AWAKENING

In the century before Spurgeon, we find what has been called the Great Awakening. The Great Awakening was a Christian growth period known in the church as revival. The Great Awakening made an impact not only in the British Isles, but in the United States also. The Great Awakening was a result of the preaching of Christian doctrine and the moving of the Holy Spirit that not only brought spiritual change, but also influenced social and political thought.

In New England, the Great Awakening began by the power of God in and through the Christian theologian and preacher Jonathan Edwards.

The Constitutional Rights Foundation says:

"In the aftermath of the Great Awakening, hundreds of new, mainly evangelical, churches formed after separating from the established

churches. The members of these new churches demanded the right to worship and preach, as they wanted. They also strongly objected to public taxes and laws that supported the established churches.

The Great Awakening created greater religious diversity and led to greater tolerance of differing religions. After the American Revolution, this tolerance was enshrined in the First Amendment to the U.S. Constitution: "Congress shall make no law respecting an establishment of religion, or prohibiting the free exercise thereof . . . ."

Some historians say that the Great Awakening was a "rehearsal" for the American Revolution. They point out that revivals used colonial newspapers, pamphlets, circulating letters, outdoor rallies, and radical oratory to create an American mass movement. Later, Sam Adams, Patrick Henry and others would use these relatively new communication techniques to unite the colonies against the king.

Those supporting the rehearsal theory also argue that evangelical preachers like James Tennent and James Davenport challenged the authority of the colonial political and religious ruling class. The New Light preachers taught Americans to decide things based on their individual consciences rather than blindly accept the will of the rich and powerful.

Hundreds of itinerant preachers carried this message of democratic individualism to the poor and powerless: women, servants, slaves, those without property, those who were uneducated, and even children. Without realizing it, say those favoring the rehearsal idea, the revivalists were preparing ordinary Americans to eventually take political matters into their own hands. Thus, the Great Awakening planted the seeds of the rebellion against England in 1776.

William H. Nelson says in his book "The American Tory":

"Throughout the colonies dissenting Protestant congregations (Congregationalist, Baptist, and Presbyterian) preached Revolutionary themes in their sermons, while most Church of England ministers preached loyalty to the King."
(The American Tory (1961) esp p. 186)

Historian Bernard Bailyn writes in "The Ideological Origins of the American Revolution":

"Puritanism ... and the epidemic evangelism of the mid-eighteenth century, had created challenges to the traditional notions of social stratification" by preaching that the Bible taught all men are equal, that the true value of a man lies in his moral behavior, not his class, and that all can be saved."
(The Ideological Origins of the American Revolution 1992 p. 273-4, 299–300)

Writer Ellis Sandoz, wrote two volumes that were titled *"Political Sermons of the American Founding Era."* Sandoz documents ministers of that day, who preached some of those sermons. One only had to read the titles to know of their political nature. This list includes:

- Benjamin Colman, Government the Pillar of the Earth
- Joseph Sewall, Nineveh's Repentance and Deliverance
- Elisha Williams, the Essential Rights and Liberties of Protestants
- George Whitefield, Britain's Mercies, and Britain's Duties
- Charles Chauncy, Civil Magistrates Must Be Just, Ruling In the Fear of God
- Samuel Davies, the Mediatorial Kingdom and Glories of Jesus Christ
- Samuel Dunbar, the Presence of God With His People
- Jonathan Mayhew, the Snare Broken
- John Joachim Zubly, an Humble Enquiry
- John Allen, an Oration Upon the Beauties of Liberty
- Isaac Backus, an Appeal to the Public For Religious Liberty
- Samuel Sherwood, Scriptural Instructions to Civil Rulers
- John Wesley, a Calm Address to Our American Colonies
- Anonymous, a Constitutional Answer to Wesley's Calm Address
- Moses Mather, America's Appeal to the Impartial World
- Samuel Sherwood, the Church's Flight Into the Wilderness: an Address On the Times
- John Witherspoon, the Dominion of Providence Over the Passions of Men
- John Fletcher, the Bible and the Sword
- Abraham Keteltas, God Arising and Pleading His People's Cause
- Jacob Cushing, Divine Judgments Upon Tyrants
- Samuel Cooper, a Sermon On the Day of the Commencement of the Constitution
- Henry Cumings, a Sermon Preached At Lexington On the 19 Th of April

If the reader looks into these messages, they will find similar things Jonathan Edwards said in a sermon in Hartford

> *"Political prosperity requires the general practice of a strict morality. But this cannot be so well secured by any other means, as by a belief of christianity. Motives of a religious kind appear to be necessary to restrain men from vice and immorality."*
> **(Jonathan Edwards)**

Congregational Pastor Samuel Wales said this in a sermon:

> *"Indeed never should it be forgotten that all the measures of civil policy ought to be founded on the great principles of religion; or, at the least, to be perfectly consistent with them: otherwise they will never be esteemed, because they will be contrary to that moral sense of right and wrong which God has implanted in the breast of every rational being."*

THE AMERICAN UPRISING

It was not long after this time, at the Virginia Convention in 1775, Patrick Henry, believing God had blessed America, made this speech:

> *Mr. President: no man thinks more highly than I do of the patriotism, as well as abilities, of the very worthy gentlemen who have just addressed the House. But different men often see the same subject in different lights; and, therefore, I hope that it will not be thought disrespectful to those gentlemen, if entertaining as I do, opinions of a character very opposite to*

theirs, I shall speak forth my sentiments freely and without reserve.

This is no time for ceremony. The question before the House is one of awful moment to this country. For my own part I consider it as nothing less than a question of freedom or slavery; and in proportion to the magnitude of the subject ought to be the freedom of the debate. It is only in this way that we can hope to arrive at truth, and fulfill the great responsibility which we hold to God and our country. Should I keep back my opinions at such a time, through fear of giving offense, I should consider myself as guilty of treason toward my country, and of an act of disloyalty toward the majesty of heaven, which I revere above all earthly things.

Mr. President, it is natural to man to indulge in the illusions of hope. We are apt to shut our eyes against a painful truth, and listen to the song of that siren, till she transforms us into beasts. Is this the part of wise men, engaged in a great and arduous struggle for liberty? Are we disposed to be of the number of those who, having eyes, see not, and having ears hear not, the things which so nearly concern their temporal salvation?

For my part, whatever anguish of spirit it may cost, I am willing to know the whole truth; to know the worst and provide for it.

I have but one lamp by which my feet are guided; and that is the lamp of experience. I know of no way of judging of the future but by the past. And judging by the past I wish to know what there has been in the conduct of the British ministry for the last ten years to justify those hopes with which gentlemen have been pleased to solace themselves and the House?

Is it that insidious smile with which our petition has been lately received? Trust it not, sir; it will prove a snare to your feet. Suffer not yourselves to be betrayed with a kiss.

Ask yourselves how this gracious reception of our petition compares with these warlike preparations which cover our waters and darken our land. Are fleets and armies necessary to a work of love and reconciliation?

Have we shown ourselves so unwilling to be reconciled, that force must be called in to win back our love?

Let us not deceive ourselves, sir. These are the implements of war and subjugation; the last arguments to which kings resort.

I ask gentlemen, sir, what means this martial array, if its purpose be not to force us to submission? Can gentlemen assign any other possible motives for it? Has Great Britain any enemy, in this quarter of the world, to call for all this accumulation of navies and armies?

No, sir, she has none. They are meant for us; they can be meant for no other. They are sent over to bind and rivet upon us those chains which the British ministry have been so long forging. And what have we to oppose them?

Shall we try argument?

Sir, we have been trying that for the past ten years. Have we anything new to offer on the subject? Nothing. We have held the subject up in every light of which it is capable; but it has all been in vain. Shall we resort to entreaty and humble supplication? What terms shall we find which have not already been exhausted?

Let us not, I beseech you, sir, deceive ourselves longer. Sir, we have done everything that could be done to avert the storm which is now coming on. We have petitioned; we have remonstrated; we have supplicated; we have prostrated ourselves before the throne, and have implored its interposition to arrest the tyrannical hands of the ministry and parliament.

Our petitions have been slighted; our remonstrances [complaints] have produced additional violence and insult; our supplications have been disregarded; and we have been spurned with contempt from the foot of the throne.

In vain, after these things, may we indulge the fond hope of peace and reconciliation. There is no longer any room for hope. If we wish to be free--- if we mean to preserve inviolate those inestimable privileges for which we have been so long contending ----if we mean not basely to abandon the noble struggle in which we have been so long engaged, and which we have pledged ourselves never to abandon until the glorious object of our contest shall be obtained, we must fight!

I repeat it, sir, we must fight! An appeal to arms and to the God of Hosts is all that is left us!

They tell us, sir, that we are weak---unable to cope with so formidable an adversary.

But when shall we be stronger? Will it be next week, or next year? Will it be when we are totally disarmed and when a British guard shall be stationed in every house?

Shall we gather strength by irresolution and inaction?...

Shall we acquire the means of effectual resistance by lying supinely on our backs, and hugging the delusive phantom of hope, until our enemies shall have bound us hand and foot?

Sir, we are not weak, if we make a proper use of those means which the God of nature hath placed in our power. Three millions of people armed in the holy cause of liberty and in such a country as that which we possess are invincible by any force which our enemy can send against us.

Besides, sir, we shall not fight our battles alone. There is a just God who presides over the destinies of nations and who will raise up friends to fight our battles for us.

The battle, sir, is not to the strong alone; it is to the vigilant, the active, the brave...

Besides, sir, we have no election. If we were base enough to desire it, it is now too late to retire from the contest. There is no retreat but in submission and slavery! Our chains are forged! Their clanking may be heard on the plains of Boston! The war is inevitable---and let it come! I repeat, sir, let it come!

It is in vain, sir, to extenuate the matter. Gentlemen may cry peace, peace---but there is no peace! The war is actually begun! The next gale that sweeps from the north will bring to our ears the clash of resounding arms!

Our brethren are already in the field!

Why stand we here idle? What is it that gentlemen wish? What would they have?

Is life so dear, or peace so sweet as to be purchased at the price of chains and slavery? Forbid it, Almighty God!

I know not what course others may take; but as for me, give me liberty or give me death!!!
(Patrick Henry)

After reading Patrick Henry's speech we may ask who influenced Henry to use the words, *"if we make a proper use of those means which the God of nature hath placed in our power. Three millions of people armed in the holy cause of liberty"* in his speech?

Writing about Patrick Henry, Isaac Backus said "Patrick Henry's mother drilled him in Christian Calvinistic theology."

Isaac Backus:

"By the time of the American Revolution, approximately two-thirds of the colonial population had been 'trained in the school of Calvin.' Henry, through his mother, was a spiritual descendant of Calvin and represented the liberating element of a Reformed theology and world-view."

This influence of Henry and other Puritans led to the words found in the Bill of Rights of the States under Constitutional Article One which states:

Congress shall make no law respecting an establishment of religion, or prohibiting the free exercise thereof; or abridging the freedom of speech, or of the press; or the right of the people peaceably to assemble, and to petition the Government for a redress of grievances.

Notice: PETITION THE GOVERNMENT FOR A REDRESS OF GRIEVANCES.

Much is said about the first part of the first amendment within the church, where it says that the government should not establish religion. Thank God that He had godly men write this document. State churches are not what the Bible has in mind. This we all agree with. However, we cannot stop there, because there is more to the amendment.

The "petitioning right" found at the end of the amendment, is just as much part of the amendment as the beginning. The same Christian minded Puritans wrote not just the beginning, but all of the words of the first amendment, and did so, in light of living under a government that had not been at peace with their faith. They wanted the church to have a voice in the government, but not have the church be ran by the government.

The first amendment not only disallows a state run church, but it also gives the church freedom to express church interests in a civil form, harnessing voting power in ways that effect change. This is the law of our land, folks and there is no greater authority other than God himself, then the Constitution in the Union States.

The non-believer has a right to petition, influence congress and harness votes for their own causes that could limit the freedom of the church. Who will make a stand in favor of peaceable time for the church? The church has a mandate from Scripture and is given the right in the Constitutional, but will it take that stand?

Those believers that want nothing to do with government, fail to see the grace God has given us in the laws that our forefathers passed. But this is not an effort to force opinion with no Biblical support. Paul gives us an example to follow.

> *Acts 16*
>
> *But when it was day, the magistrates sent the police, saying, "Let those men go." And the jailer reported these words to Paul, saying, "The magistrates have sent to let you go. Therefore come out now and go in peace." But Paul said to them, "They have beaten us publicly, uncondemned, men who are Roman citizens, and have thrown us into prison; and do they now throw us out secretly? No! Let them come themselves and take us out." The police reported these words to the magistrates, and they were afraid when they heard that they were Roman citizens. So they came and apologized to them. And they took them out and asked them to leave the city. So they went out of the prison and visited Lydia. And when they had seen the brothers, they encouraged them and departed.*

In this passage Paul stood up to the magistrates' authority. Paul could have just walked away and have said, this has nothing to do with the gospel. But within the God ordained government, Paul used his right as a

Roman citizen to demand justice. Paul used the government law again in Acts 22 when he said to the centurion who was standing by, *"Is it lawful for you to flog a man who is a Roman citizen and uncondemned?"*

God has established the civil authorities and we are to honor them. Government is God ordained to establish order in society and to provide for the common good for mankind. The laws of the government are also God ordained, if the law does not try to over rule the Law of God, then we the church, as Paul directed, should use the law for the betterment of the church.

> *Psalm 106: 3*
> *Blessed are they who observe justice, who do righteousness at all times!*

We are not only to pray for our leaders, but also we are to influence them to do right in the eyes of God, working within the laws of the ordained government that God has placed us under.

4) A CITY ON A HILL

Matthew 5:13-14
"You are the salt of the earth, but if salt has lost its taste, how shall its saltiness be restored? It is no longer good for anything except to be thrown out and trampled under people's feet. "You are the light of the world. A city set on a hill cannot be hidden.

John MacArthur said

" the United States was actually born out of a violation of the New Testament principles, and any blessings that God has bestowed on America have come in spite of that disobedience by the Founding Fathers" (From: Why Government Can't save You)

WAS PATRICK HENRY'S SPEECH A SIN?

Some may agree with John MacArthur, saying this was a blatant sin. Surely all Christians agree it was Divine Providence that brought about the design of this nation, even if one were to view Patrick Henry's acts as sin. Do we not say the same of Joseph and his brothers?

> Genesis 50: 16-20
> So they sent a message to Joseph, saying, "Your father gave this command before he died, 'Say to Joseph, Please forgive the transgression of your brothers and their sin, because they did evil to you.' And now, please forgive the transgression of the servants of the God of your father." Joseph wept when they spoke to him. His brothers also came and fell down before him and said, "Behold, we are your servants." But Joseph said to them, "Do not fear, for am I in the place of God? As for you, you meant evil against me, but God meant it for good, to bring it about that many people should be kept alive, as they are today.

God used the evil will and sin of Joseph's brothers to bring about His good will. If God is in control, are we not demanded to see God's will in Patrick Henry's actions? But notice also, that the good found here is based upon the premise "That many people should be kept alive." The whole culture, not just believers, benefit from God's plan. Abraham Kuyper's teaching on common grace comes to mind here.

Patrick Henry was a founder of this nation that stood with other Reformed believers making Christian statements in government meeting halls, in front of political leaders of his day, because he saw God calling him to make an impact on his government. Many more examples from history could be given. It would be foolish to deny that Christians of the past, did indeed feel compelled to openly influence the government for the good of the church. It would also be foolish to say the church did not benefit from the stands that Patrick Henry and others made.

The question still remains, does our faith allow such involvement?

I will argue from two standpoints and say most definitely yes, Christians should be involved. The first will be the Reformed traditional position, and the second which will follow in Chapter 5, will be Christian's final authority, Scripture itself.

HISTORY SUPPORTED ORTHODOXICAL VIEW

From nearly the beginning days in Geneva, the Reformed Church has taken a consistent approach to these matters. The consistent teaching on this, is why we have so many examples to pull from in history. Maybe the best way to express the Reformed position, is to follow the teaching of Richard Niebuhr, "Christ and Culture" (1951).

Niebuhr narrates the history of the church and how Christianity has responded to cultures from different segments. He outlines five prevalent viewpoints running from one extreme to the other.

CHRIST AGAINST CULTURE

In this viewpoint, church parishioners are encouraged to remove themselves, as much as one humanly can, from culture. Examples of this would be the hyper-separatist groups such as the Amish, Mennonites, Monks, Convent Nuns, and to a lesser extent you see this in the Hyper-Fundamentalists. They view all of culture as evil and believers must not have anything to do with it in any area, for fear of corruption.

CHRIST OF CULTURE

This is pretty much the Liberal view of the role of the church in culture. According to Liberals, the church is to adjust to the Culture it finds itself in. This allows Liberals to change such things as the church's view of gay marriage. In other words, since the Culture now view gay marriage as okay, the church should too.

Niebuhr has three other viewpoints that rest between the extremes, that are more Biblical than the others.

CHRIST ABOVE CULTURE

All of culture is not all evil. Culture is founded on the naturally created good of God, and although nature and culture are fallen, they are still subject to God. Thomas Aquinas held to this view. Aquinas believed the church must be viewed as simultaneously in and beyond the world, leading people to salvation in heaven yet encouraging all that is found good in this world's culture. From this came the great ideas of general education and protective legislation for all citizens.

CHRIST AND CULTURE IN PARADOX

The paradox view is not the same as Christ above Culture in that while both Christ and culture claim our loyalty, the tension between them cannot be reconciled by any lasting synthesis. There is a major contrast between two realms: the left-hand realm of the world governed by law and the right-hand realm of God governed by grace. These two realms exist side by side in a paradoxical relation, never to be resolved in this life.

CHRIST TRANSFORMING CULTURE

This last viewpoint is similar to the preceding except that it is more optimistic about the ability of Christians to improve culture. This view, I believe, is the most biblical and God honoring. History is the story of God's mighty deeds and humanity's response to them. Those that hold this view are often called Conversionists. Conversionists live in the divine "now" and as culture changes we change with the culture, until the culture goes against biblical truths.

Look at TV as one example. At one time, we had no TV to influence the culture. Now the TV stays on in many homes, most of the time that the family is there. There is much influence coming to us through the TV. Now, what do we do about this, if that influence is bad? After all, TV is not talked about in Scripture.

The Christ against Culture would remove all TVs because there are bad shows being aired. The

Conversionists would not remove the TV, but turn it off when bad shows come on, and work in the culture to encourage Christian friendly shows.

If change is toward evil, the Conversionists work to transform it back to God's will. Why do this? The Conversionists know that, as seen in the past, there are huge benefits to the church and the culture by having a Political Christian nation.

This is not to say we are building a Christian state church or even a Christian TV network. The goal is to have a peaceable environment for the faith. One example of this is whereas a Christian should never belong to a Mormon church, a Christian could easily support a Mormon for public office. This is not aligning with Mormons in theology, but realizing that a Mormon would be in favor of laws that would allow the church to live in peace with its government.

One of the fundamental theological reasons for this optimism is the view that the Fall perverted things which God had created as good. God's word is capable of reforming all things including government, even if they reject the Son as their Savor. It is not that mankind can by its own efforts create a more holy culture, but that through the action of God's grace, a respect to God is laid on the culture. Augustine was impressed by Caesar-centered Rome as a "Christian city." Calvin emphasized the use of God's Law as a social reformer. Since then, Christians have typically been even more optimistic than Calvin himself along these lines.

We again point to the Puritanism of England and American and add Abraham Kuyper in Holland as examples of Christ transforming culture.

Christian schools

God allowed my wife and I to send our daughters to Christian schools. Therefore, I am a huge supporter of Christian schools. However, one negative side effect of this, is when Christians pulled their children from public schools, they no longer paid much attention to the public school system. The lessened Christian influence seen now in public schools, allowing more atheism to come in.

This is not saying that no Christians remained in the public school system. Thank God there are many that do battle each day with the forces of the dark kingdom in our schools. Nor is it saying that the Christian school movement should be abandoned. Rather, it is a call for Christian tax payers, that currently have their children in Christian schools to not forget about the public schools. We should not wash our hands of public schools and be done with it, for that's what the Devil wants. If God has allowed you to send your children to Christian school, praise God for that blessing, but remember the battle remains in the public school. Good schools are good for our culture and the church.

This same decay is seen in liberal denominational history. Once the conservative theologian (salt) pulled away from these liberal denominations to start their own, nothing restrained liberal theology from drifting into full decay.

The Orthodoxical view for the church in society

The Orthodoxical view for the church in society can be summed up this way. When God placed man in the Garden of Eden, he gave man a cultural mandate.

> *Genesis 1:28*
> *"Be fruitful and multiply and fill the earth and subdue it and have dominion over the fish of the sea and over the birds of the heavens and over every living thing that moves on the earth."*

Adam and Eve were called to serve as God's vice regents over the world. They were to manage the earth in all things thereby bringing glory to God. From the Reformed view, this mandate has not been set aside, but it is reiterated throughout Scripture. The gospel mandate that Christ gave his church was designed to redeem man from sin, so that this cultural mandate may be fulfilled.

Because of this, Reformed theology teaches that every aspect of life, must be brought under the Lordship of Christ. Reformed theology rejects the idea that some aspects of life are religious while others are secular. All of life is religious and being governed by either the true religion or a false religion. The arts, the sciences, law, politics, business, family, sports, school and every aspect of our life should fall under the truth of the gospel. That truth is Christ is Lord of all things. This is what brings glory to God.

This, I believe, is the message of Matthew 5, "A City on a Hill"

> *"You are the salt of the earth, but if salt has lost its taste, how shall its saltiness be restored? It is no longer good for anything except to be thrown out and trampled under people's feet.*

"You are the light of the world. A city set on a hill cannot be hidden. Nor do people light a lamp and put it under a basket, but on a stand, and it gives light to all in the house. In the same way, let your light shine before others, so that they may see your good works and give glory to your Father who is in heaven.

You are the salt of the earth, but if salt has lost its taste, how shall its saltiness be restored? It is no longer good for anything except to be thrown out and trampled under people's feet.

The good is the effort we are to use in changing our world for the good of the Kingdom/church. It is the idea of restraining evil as we said before. This passage says, if we do not do this, we are worthless to the Kingdom.

In verse 16 Jesus uses the word "good" again.

In the same way, let your light shine before others, so that they may see your good works and give glory to your Father who is in heaven.

CULTURE MANDATE VS EVANGELICAL MANDATE

The Cultural Mandate is not the same as the Great Commission. The Cultural Mandate is actions taken by the church to change society not just for the good of the church, but for the good of all people. The Great Commission or Evangelical Mandate is the power and presence of God that changes hearts. No Christian would dare say that the Cultural Mandate is the foremost goal of the church. Evangelical efforts are and should always be the top duty of the believer. However, the Evangelical Mandate did not abrogate the Cultural Mandate. Yet many wish to forget or ignore the Cultural

Mandate when the Cultural Mandate is a great benefit to the Evangelical Mandate.

5) THE CHRISTIAN HANDBOOK

"..let your light shine before others, so that they may see your good works and give glory to your Father who is in heaven"

This idea of good works is found throughout Scripture. Salvation has nothing to do with good works, but clearly our Lord wants believers to work for the good of the church. In fact, Ephesians 2:10 says this is the reason God saved us.

We are his workmanship, FOR THE REASON OF GOOD WORKS.

Eph. 2: 10
For we are his workmanship, created in Christ Jesus for good works, which God prepared beforehand, that we should walk in them.

Our good works are to be seen in public, not just within the walls of church. While the believer is to separate from the world on one hand, he is to support all causes that seek to promote the social, economic, political, and educational welfare of the community. Paul says in Galatians,

> *"And let us not grow weary of doing good, for in due season we will reap, if we do not give up. So then, as we have opportunity, let us do good to everyone, and especially to those who are of the household of faith."*

In case you didn't pick up on it, Paul said "especially to those who are of the household of faith," which means that when he said "do good to everyone," this includes those outside the church.

Pushing for a Christian culturally aligned environment is good for all mankind. Those that would have us split our lives into part secular and part Christian, will not find support in Scripture. Scripture teaches unity of the church.

The church is to be unified not lean toward individuality

> *Romans 15:5-6*
> *5 Now may the God of patience and comfort grant you to be like-minded toward one another, according to Christ Jesus, 6 that you may with one mind and one mouth glorify the God and Father of our Lord Jesus Christ.*

This unity is found in Christ's High Priestly prayer of John 17. There are a number of points we should look at in this passage, so I will start at verse 16

John 17: 16-22
They are not of the world, just as I am not of the world. Sanctify them in the truth; your word is truth. 18 As you sent me into the world, so I have sent them into the world. And for their sake I consecrate myself, that they also may be sanctified in truth. "I do not ask for these only, but also for those who will believe in me through their word, that they may all be one, just as you, Father, are in me, and I in you, that they also may be in us, so that the world may believe that you have sent me. The glory that you have given me I have given to them, that they may be one even as we are one,

Notice the phrase *"that they may all be one, just as you, Father, are in me, and I in you"* and also the phrase *"that they may be one even as we are one."*

Those that would divide the believers into parts, the church and the individual, are really asking the believer to be more of a Christian out of the church as the invisible church, than inside it's walls as they become the visible church. They say it is fine for the individual to speak on cultural issues on their own, but when gathered, we should remain quiet. There is little difference from the politician that declares he is personally against abortion, but supports the argument that laws should not limit the nation's own choice on the matter.

There is only one reason to disagree with abortion. Here is an excerpt I wrote for a newspaper article:

"Deep to the root of the debate, there are not a handful of reasons to oppose an abortion.

There is, in fact, only one reason. If you personally do not agree with abortion, it would not be because you see the baby as mere tissue. It all hinges on one base aspect from which all the other issues sprout. So there is no good reason to personally oppose abortion unless you believe that one element to be true. That element is that the baby is a created life, a person whom there is no need to kill.

To say you are "personally" for life, but care not if others choose to take a life is but a sham to the highest degree. The propaganda of this rationale is indeed a fraudulent claim and must be exposed for what it is. Stop trying to fool people who see your true colors. You cannot have it both ways."

If there is any good found in the individual believer to oppose abortion, then that good should be proclaimed in the church where Christians gather. This can be carried across all issues in our culture. To say that the church should not get involved in cultural issues is simply wrong.

Notice also in the John 17 the phrase:

As you sent me (Christ) into the world, so I have sent them (followers of Christ) into the world.

Christ sent his followers into the world. We, too, are sent into the world. The pastor of each church is first to teach the saints and then send the saints to share to the world.

2 Timothy 4:

> *2preach the word; be ready in season and out of season; reprove, rebuke, and exhort, with complete patience and teaching. 3 For the time is coming when people will not endure sound teaching, but having itching ears they will accumulate for themselves teachers to suit their own passions, 4and will turn away from listening to the truth and wander off into myths.*

All believers are to be in the word of God. But let's face it, many do not follow this standard. Many only open their Bibles on Sunday morning. If abortion is wrong, who will tell these believers that do not read the Bible as they should, that it is wrong? Will the world tell them this?

If it is good for an individual believer to speak against certain issues, then it is also good for the pastor who opposes a particular issue to let the church know of his opposition. Why gag the pastor on cultural issues, when he is to lead the flock to transform all of life? Is it not the duty of those who sit in the pews, the ones that will be sent out to share that transforming power to the evil world?

We are indeed in a war. (The book of Ephesians)

The Christian faith sees the book of Ephesians as a handbook about and for the church. The book begins with a praise to our Great King and tells us the work God has done, to bring us together as one, through Christ. In chapter 1, God built His church, by choosing us (vs 4), predestinating us (vs 5), by adopting us (vs 5), by making us accepted (vs 6), by redeeming us (vs 7), and by forgiving us (vs 7).

Now please notice this. Ephesians 1 says we are brought into the church *"to unite all things in him, things in heaven and things on earth"* (vs 10). This is God's work, and it gives insight into God's plan.

I see this as the same cultural mandate found in Genesis 1.

> *28 And God blessed them. And God said to them, "Be fruitful and multiply and fill the earth and subdue it and have dominion over the fish of the sea and over the birds of the heavens and over every living thing that moves on the earth."*

The first Adam failed in this mandate. Christ, who is the second Adam, has an effectual plan in gathering all things to Himself. Later in chapter 4 we will see that all believers are to work toward this same Oneness that God has planned from the beginning.

William Barclay paraphrases this passage:

> *"The secret was a purpose which he formed in his own mind before time began, so that the periods of time should be controlled and administered until they reached their full development, a development in which all things, in heaven and upon earth, are gathered into one in Jesus Christ" (Ephesians 1:8-10, Barclay's paraphrase)*

Salvation is an individual matter between God and the individual. Because of salvation, we, the elect of God, are gathered as one body, under One Head, with the mandate of working for the glory of God. The glory of God is found in making God's Son Lord of all things.

The teaching of the headship of Christ is referred to often in the New Testament, and it refers to His authority and rule. The purpose of God in history is to bring glory to Himself by bringing all of creation under the headship (the authority and rule) of Christ. This truth is taught in a number of other New Testament passages.

Colossians 1:15-20

15He is the image of the invisible God, the firstborn of all creation. 16For by him all things were created, in heaven and on earth, visible and invisible, whether thrones or dominions or rulers or authorities—all things were created through him and for him. 17And he is before all things, and in him all things hold together. 18And he is the head of the body, the church. He is the beginning, the firstborn from the dead, that in everything he might be preeminent. 19For in him all the fullness of God was pleased to dwell, 20and through him to reconcile to himself all things, whether on earth or in heaven, making peace by the blood of his cross.

The message of Colossians 1, is the message the church must proclaim to the world. This message does not stop at the door of a government facility. Romans 13 tells us that God is over government, because the government's authority comes from God.

1Let every person be subject to the governing authorities. For there is no authority except from God, and those that exist have been instituted by God.

The proclamation and explanation of God's plan to bring all things under the Lordship of Christ was a part of Paul's special calling and a commission given him by God as seen in Ephesians 3: 7-13

> 7Of this gospel I was made a minister according to the gift of God's grace, which was given me by the working of his power. 8To me, though I am the very least of all the saints, this grace was given, to preach to the Gentiles the unsearchable riches of Christ, 9and to bring to light for everyone what is the plan of the mystery hidden for ages in God who created all things, 10so that through the church the manifold wisdom of God might now be made known to the rulers and authorities in the heavenly places. 11This was according to the eternal purpose that he has realized in Christ Jesus our Lord, 12in whom we have boldness and access with confidence through our faith in him. 13So I ask you not to lose heart over what I am suffering for you, which is your glory.

While chapter 1 of Ephesians looked at our salvation from God's standpoint, chapter 2 of Ephesians tells how we as individuals (the invisible church) have been drawn from the kingdom of darkness, and gathered into the Church from man's viewpoint. We are no longer strangers to the church, but now saints within the church. We walked after this world, in the dark kingdom, but now sit with Christ in heavenly places. We once were dead in sin, but now within the church we have been made alive together with Christ.

This unity (together with Christ) is not limited to our relationship with Jesus. Yes, Christ is the Head of the church, but there are also other parts of the body. The rest of the body are the saints of the church. This is what Paul addresses in chapter 3 of Ephesians.

In Chapter 3 Paul talks about groups of people being united in the church. This union I see best played out in the visible church. In other words, as much as it is a mystery for God to bring people together from all walks of life, once the church gathers locally, something even more amazing happens that is puzzling even to the angels in Heaven.

> *Ephesians 3:10*
> *so that through the church the manifold wisdom of God might now be made known to the rulers and authorities in the heavenly places.*

The other nations have always been looked at as heathen, with no special blessing from God. After all God had referred to the Jewish nation many times in the Old testament as "My people," which means that others are not his people. If this mystery be true of the invisible church, it is even more true of the visible church. Jewish believers now gather together in the same local church with other nations whom they once hated.

This, Paul says, is the mystery of the church. The mystery is how God can take different groups of people from all over the world and bring them together as one. Paul says this is the message that he preaches to everyone.

Ephesians 3: 8-9
8To me, though I am the very least of all the saints, this grace was given, to preach to the Gentiles the unsearchable riches of Christ, 9and to bring to light for everyone what is the plan of the mystery hidden for ages in God who created all things,

This short survey of Ephesians is the background used to address chapter 4.

In classic Pauline style, Paul begins with teaching the truth in doctrine (Ephesians chapters 1-3), and follows by application (Ephesians 4-6).

In chapter 4 Paul tells how we should take this truth and apply it to our "walk." The walk, as I'm sure you know, is our daily life as a believer. While at home, work, school, job, etc.

Ephesians 4:1
I therefore, a prisoner for the Lord, urge you to walk in a manner worthy of the calling to which you have been called,

Paul says that our walk begins with humility of self, no longer an individual, but rather acting as one with the church. We are One body, with One Spirit, one hope, One Lord, one faith, one baptism, and One God.

Paul makes it very clear that he is talking about the visible church here as he writes in verses 11-12:

11And he gave the apostles, the prophets, the evangelists, the shepherds and teachers, 12 to equip the saints for the work of ministry, for building up the body of Christ

Shepherds/pastors are not over the whole invisible church, but rather, over the local visible church. The teaching that the pastor gives is for the local church.

Chapter 4 verse 17 and begins a list of truths the pastor is to teach the church in how it should walk in Christ.

4:17 no longer walk as the Gentiles do, in the futility of their minds

4: 19 Don't be greedy.

4: 22 put off self and renew your minds with the Spirit.

4: 24 Take on God's righteousness and holiness

4: 25 Speak the truth of God's righteousness and holiness to others.

4: 26 Get anger under control.

4: 28 Don't be a thief, but work with your hands, in order to share with others.

4: 29 Watch what comes from your mouth.

4: 30 Don't grieve the Holy Spirit.

4: 32 don't be bitter or malicious.

4: 31 Be kind.

5: 1 Imitate God.

5: 2 walk in love.

5: 3-5 be pure.

To sum it all up, Paul comes to verse 6 of chapter 5.

> *Ephesians 5*
> *6 Let no one deceive you with empty words, for because of these things the wrath of God comes upon the sons of disobedience. 7Therefore do not become partners with them; 8for at one time you were darkness, but now you are light in the Lord. Walk as children of light 9(for the fruit of light is found in all that is good and right and true),*

I want to key in on the words, *"partners,"* *"fruit of light,"* and *"all that is good and true."*

Again I remind others, if an individual pastor believes it is good to stand against issues such as gay marriage, that same pastor should teach his church that good truth.

The church is commanded to oppose the dark Kingdom in all areas. This includes those who live as ambassadors of the evil kingdom working to influence leaders in a cause against the church. We are not to partner with the Kingdom of darkness, and it should be noted that, we do partner with them when we take on an attitude of apathy. Those in the Kingdom of light (the church) are the fruit of light. In other words the church is the ambassador of the light that teaches the goodness of God, and upholds righteousness and truth.

Paul emphasized this further in the next verse.

> *Ephesians 5...*
> *10 and try to discern what is pleasing to the Lord.*

Just in case you didn't get it, in verse 11, Paul makes this as clear as possible.   11Take no part in the unfruitful works of darkness, but instead expose them.

This is not a passive battle, but an aggressive one. We are not to wait until the sin comes into the church, but rather if we see seeds of sin being planted within our area in which we have been called to be ambassadors of the light, we are to expose the evil in those that wish to reside in the kingdom of darkness. Notice that this even regards the things that they do in secret.

> *12For it is shameful even to speak of the things that they do in secret.*

Some in the kingdom of darkness, say that what the church views as sin is a private matter. However, Scripture says the Kingdom of light (the Church) is to expose this as sin.

Paul, next gives the church a code of living for husband and wife, children and parents and those within your domestic community. Then we come to verse 10 of chapter 6, there Paul paints a very graphic picture of this warfare.

10Finally, be strong in the Lord and in the strength of his might. 11 Put on the whole armor of God, that you may be able to stand against the schemes of the devil. 12For we do not wrestle against flesh and blood, but against the rulers, against the authorities, against the cosmic powers over this present darkness, against the spiritual forces of evil in the heavenly places. 13Therefore take up the whole armor of God, that you may be able to withstand in the evil day, and having done all, to stand firm. 14Stand therefore, having fastened on the belt of truth, and having put on the breastplate of righteousness, 15and, as shoes for your feet, having put on the readiness given by the gospel of peace. 16In all circumstances take up the shield of faith, with which you can extinguish all the flaming darts of the evil one; 17and take the helmet of salvation, and the sword of the Spirit, which is the word of God, 18praying at all times in the Spirit, with all prayer and supplication. To that end keep alert with all perseverance, making supplication for all the saints, 19and also for me, that words may be given to me in opening my mouth boldly to proclaim the mystery of the gospel, 20for which I am an ambassador in chains, that I may declare it boldly, as I ought to speak.

Notice this phrase, *"having done all, to stand firm."*

Having done (Strong's 2716) (katergazomai [word study] from katá = intensifies meaning of verb + ergazomai = work or engage in an activity involving considerable expenditure of effort) means to work out fully and thoroughly, to accomplish or achieve an end, to finish or carry something to its conclusion.

So, we are not only to stand firm throughout our life time, but we are to fully carry it out in all areas of life.

Calvin said of this passage:

> They are thus directed to cherish confidence through the whole course of life. There will be no danger which may not be successfully met by the power of God; nor will any who, with this assistance, fight against Satan, fail in the day of battle.

Puritan writer William Gurnall says:

> In heaven we shall appear, not in armor, but in robes of glory. But here these are to be worn night and day; we must walk, work, and sleep in them, or else we are not true soldiers of Christ...We must not confide in the armor of God, but in the God of this armor, because all our weapons are only "mighty through God".

William Barclay says that the word, katergazomai,
> "always has the idea of bringing to completion..."carry to its perfect conclusion."

We must live in light of the fact that just as much as "God loves the church and died for her, " so it is true that Satan hates the church and sends evil to hamper the good! Satan is always willing to enlist men that will work in his will of bringing evil upon mankind. This comes from not only non-believers given over to Satan, but from believers in a state of apathy. The reality in which we must always live is that the church has an enemy who wishes nothing but evil for us and who does not rest or grow weary in seeking to accomplish this objective.

Many see the supernatural in this passage, (Ephesians 6) without understanding the reality in which it is manifested. Paul is reminding us that there are indeed greater powers behind the scenes in the Kingdom, but they are manifested in real life, in real events that we all face. In other words, Paul is not saying that we fight invisible battles, but rather the evil battles we fight are being influenced and empowered by something greater than the people that stand in opposition to the church. This understanding, is what Paul wants us to carry in our relationship with our spouse, our relationship with our offspring, and our relationship in our domestic community and in all areas of life. Therefore, Paul is telling us to stand firm, as saints of God, for we are in full battle in all places.

How far do we take this?

Paul says we must do all that we can. If the city wants to pass laws that will allow more strip bars in the city, we as a church must see this as the work of the Dark Kingdom and do all that we can to oppose it for the Kingdom of light. If the government wants to pass laws to provide government funding of abortion, we as a church must see this as the work of the Devil, and do all that we can to stop it. You may ask, "Do you mean preach against cultural issues in a message on Sundays?" Yes, for ministers are to preach the Word, and instruct in ALL righteousness.

> *2 Timothy 3:16*
> *All scripture is given by inspiration of God, and is profitable for doctrine, for reproof, for correction, for instruction in righteousness:*

Again some would claim this is for the individual, but not for the local church. I mentioned John Frame's quote early and repeat it here.

> *Now some have argued that cultural transformation is the work of Christian individuals, but not of the local church. They argue that the latter should be limited to the area of the "spiritual," the preaching of the gospel and the administration of the sacraments. But the spiritual/ secular distinction is not biblical. The gospel as proclaimed by John (Matt. 3:2), Jesus (Matt. 4:17), Philip (Acts 8:12), and Paul (Acts 19:8, 20:25, 28:23, 28:31) announces the coming of the kingdom of God, a new order of righteousness, peace, and joy (Rom. 14:17). In the kingdom, we do all things (not just "spiritual") to the glory of God (1 Cor. 10:31), all things in the name of the Lord Jesus (Col. 3:17). It is plain that care for the poor, orphans, and widows is part of that.*

Dr. Martyn Lloyd-Jones used William Wilberforce as a model that the church and the individual are not the same. Maybe Lloyd-Jones didn't know everything about Wilberforce.

ChristianHistory.net says this of William Wilberforce:

Slavery was only one cause that excited Wilberforce's passions. His second great calling was for the "reformation of manners," that is, morals. In early 1787, he conceived of a society that would work, as a royal proclamation put it, "for the encouragement of piety and virtue; and for the preventing of vice, profaneness, and immorality."

In fact, Wilberforce—dubbed "the prime minister of a cabinet of philanthropists"—was at one time active in support of 69 philanthropic causes. He gave away one-quarter of his annual income to the poor. He fought on behalf of chimney sweeps, single mothers, Sunday schools, orphans, and juvenile delinquents. He helped found para-church groups like the Society for Bettering the Cause of the Poor, the Church Missionary Society, the British and Foreign Bible Society, and the Antislavery Society.

In 1797, he settled at Clapham, where he became a prominent member of the "Clapham Sect," a group of devout Christians of influence in government and business. That same year he wrote Practical View of the Prevailing Religious System of Professed Christians—a scathing critique of comfortable Christianity that became a bestseller.

WHO INFLUENCED WILLIAM WILBERFORCE?

Wilberforce's spiritual journey started when he read "The Rise and Progress of Religion in the Soul" by Calvinist writer Philip Doddridge. Wilberforce sought guidance from Christian John Newton, who was a leading Evangelical Anglican clergyman and Rector of the day. Newton counseled Wilberforce to remain in politics, and he resolved to do so with increased diligence and conscientiousness."

What is this? A church leader influencing a politician to the good of the church? Yes, indeed.

Wilberforce's political views were formed by his faith and the close relationship he had with his minister John Newton. He then desired to promote Christianity and Christian ethics in private and public life.

6) UNDERSTANDING ROMANS 13: 1-7

Romans 13 is the flagship passage for those who believe the Christian church should not take a stand against an ungodly government, but leave it in the Lords hands. The verses in particular that seem to hold the most weight are verses 1 and 2.

> *Romans 13*
> *1 Let every person be subject to the governing authorities. For there is no authority except from God, and those that exist have been instituted by God. 2 Therefore whoever resists the authorities resists what God has appointed, and those who resist will incur judgment.*

Admittedly these verses can read as some say they do, and disallow all church's condescending voices to ward their government. However, I do not feel it is the best way to read these verse. Therefore we must spend time looking at just what is said in context.

We have already seen that from a study of the America political history, that as a Republic our nation is unlike any other nation. Our Republic has smaller republics of 50 states within a Union.

Each of these states was intended to exercise sovereignty within its own jurisdiction, and was never placed under the jurisdiction of the Federal government in Washington, D.C., which existed merely as a servant of the Union. According to the rulings of Glass v. The Sloop Betsy in 1794 and Harcourt v. Gaillard in 1827:

> *Our government was founded upon compact. Sovereignty was, and is, in the people [of the states]. (Glass v. The Sloop Betsy (1794), 3 Dall. 6)*

> *Each [state] declared itself sovereign and independent, according to the limits of its territory. (Harcourt v. Gaillard (1827), 25 U.S. 12 Wheat)*

However, more can be said about this passage. We should look at the more common views.

UNQUESTIONING SUBJECTION VIEW

One group sees this passage as a divine sanction of non-resisting and unquestioning subjection to civil authority to whatever comes down the pike. In this view, rulers may be ungodly, tyrannical, immoral and still yet God wants Christians to do nothing but endure the ungodliness. The rulers may remove liberties and rights of the people, and Christians are to do nothing but pray for them. Now, Christians do not need to actively support the immoral and ungodliness but simply be in a passive obedience through non-resistance. This they say is how God would have us handle this ungodly civil environment. Or else, "those who resist will incur judgment."

In 1660 England had a group made up mainly of high Episcopacy churches that held this view. They saw this passage as support for the right of leaders to force their subjects into submission with no regard for their human rights. However, most found it impossible to carry out this view of Romans 13 consistantly.

According to James Willson:

> When James II attempted to lay violent hands upon its chartered rights and immunities, Oxford resisted: it ate its own words, and took rank with the most decided adversaries of that Popish king in his assaults upon English Law and Protestantism. While power was in the hands of a court professedly Protestant, and zealous for the ecclesiastical supremacy of the Church of England, it was all well enough; but when a new government arose which sought to transfer all the posts of honor and influence in church and state into popish hands, these conscientious defenders of an absolute divine right took the alarm, and refused to be bound by their own repeatedly asserted doctrines. ((Civil Government/An Exposition of Romans 13: 1–7 / 3rd Millennium Ministries)James McLeod Willson, Professor of Theology at Allegheny Seminary)

This interpretation not only lacks strong historical support but also exegetical support. The Reformation was not just against the Pope but also a disobedience to the "governing authorities" of the Emperor who demanded submission to the Roman Catholic church.

The Diet of Worms was a decree issued on May 25, 1521 by Emperor Charles V which declared:

> For this reason we forbid anyone from this time forward to dare, either by words or by deeds, to receive, defend, sustain, or favour the said Martin Luther. On the contrary, we want him to be apprehended and punished as a notorious heretic, as he deserves, to be brought personally before us, or to be securely guarded until those who have captured him inform us, where upon we will order the appropriate manner of proceeding against the said Luther. Those who will help in his capture will be rewarded generously for their good work.

When it was demanded of Martin Luther at the Diet of Worms to recant of his opposition to papal authority, he replied:

> Unless I am refuted and convicted by testimonies of the Scriptures or by clear arguments... I am conquered by the Holy Scriptures quoted by me, and my conscience is bound in the word of God: I can not and will not recant any thing, since it is unsafe and dangerous to do any thing against the conscience. Here I stand. God help me! Amen.
> **(Martin Luther)**

Luther's stand against tyranny literally set off the Protestant Reformation.

Church historian, Philip Schaff:

> Luther's testimony before the Diet is an event of world-historical importance and far-reaching effect. It opened an intellectual conflict which is still going on in the civilized world. He stood there as the fearless champion of the supremacy of the word of God over the traditions of men, and of the liberty of conscience over the tyranny of authority....
>
> When tradition becomes a wall against freedom, when authority degenerates into tyranny, the very blessing is turned into a curse, and history is threatened with stagnation and death. At such rare junctures, Providence raises those pioneers of progress, who have the intellectual and moral courage to break through the restraints at the risk of their lives, and to open new paths for the onward march of history.... Conscience is the voice of God in man. It is his most sacred possession. No power can be allowed to stand between the gift and the giver. Even an erring conscience must be respected, and cannot be forced.

We have a number of Scripture texts that tell of believers standing against governing authorities. Jesus, in Matthew 21:12-13, took a whip to the governing authorities of the temple for allowing it used as a market place. Hebrew midwives defied Pharaoh, the then governing authority, to preserve the life of the infant Moses (Exodus 1:15-22). Rahab hid Joshua's spies who were conducting reconnaissance for the governing authorities in Jerico (Joshua 2:1-14). Daniel declined food from governing authorities, fit for a king (Daniel 1:8-21) and did not cease to pray when he was told not to by governing authorities (Daniel 6). Daniel's friends (Shadrach, Meshach, and Abed-Nego) refused to bow to the king's image that governing authorities set up (Daniel 3:1-30). Jesus healed on the Sabbath and that displeased governing authorities (Luke 6:6-11, 14:1-6).

Then we have Paul,

Acts 16:36-40

36 And the jailer reported these words to Paul, saying, "The magistrates have sent to let you go. Therefore come out now and go in peace." 37 But Paul said to them, "They have beaten us publicly, uncondemned, men who are Roman citizens, and have thrown us into prison; and do they now throw us out secretly? No! Let them come themselves and take us out." 38 The police reported these words to the magistrates, and they were afraid when they heard that they were Roman citizens. 39 So they came and apologized to them. And they took them out and asked them to leave the city. 40 So they went out of the prison and visited Lydia. And when they had seen the brothers, they encouraged them and departed.

It should be clear to every one that non-resisting and unquestioning subjection to civil authority is not what was meant by Paul in Romans 13.

THE EXCEPTIONS VIEW

The more common view of this passage follows the principle of non-resisting and unquestioning subjection as indicated above, but with an allowable exception. This exception is, if any issue goes against a godly, Bible based conscience and conflicts with the laws of God, a believer cannot follow them. When a conflict comes according to this view, resisting is then allowed.

While I believe this is a better view and more Biblical than the first, there is still a major problem with it. The text alone does not allow for exceptions. It is rather emphatic about the subject. The text says, Let every person be subject to the governing authorities, and those that are not subject and resist, will be judged by the wrath of God (Wrath of God comes later in the text).

THREAT TO GOOD VIEW

Another way to read this text is to see that the passage limits the governing authorities duties within the passage itself.

In this way, when Paul wrote of the authorities which are "appointed by God," it was for - the duty of being "not a terror to good works, but to evil" (verse 3). Paul then described the primary function of the governing authorities in verse 4:

> Romans 13:4,
> "For the one in authority is God's servant for your good. But if you do wrong, be afraid, for rulers do not bear the sword for no reason. They

are God's servants, agents of wrath to bring punishment on the wrongdoer."

Viewing it this way, the passage is only a reference to the punishment of criminals, who are external threats to the society. Beyond these duties, the civil magistrate has no authority granted to him by God.

The problem with this view, is that Paul and Jesus were threats to their society and would have been in sin if this view were true.

WHAT I SEE AS THE BEST VIEW

Another way to see this is that the passage is part of the Culture Mandate of Scripture. The passage can be divided into three sections.

Section 1: Paul's Proposition - Verses 1
Section 2: Paul's Argument - Verses 2-5
Section 3: Paul's Main Meaning of the phrase:
    "being subject to"- verses 6-7

Paul's Proposition

Let everyone be subject to the governing authorities, for there is no authority except that which God has established. The authorities that exist have been established by God.

To understand Paul's point here we need to understand that God is a God of order. In six days God ordered the universe into existence going from a state of chaos to paradise. We are reminded of how orderly the universe is when something like a hurricane reigns chaos on our world.

There is no reason from a naturalistic standpoint why hurricanes and other catastrophes should not reign chaos upon us continually. However, this is not what we see. God has placed gravity and other forces to hold things together.

Why is there gravity? This has been asked of many scientists with most of the answers given sounding something like this one:

I wish I knew, but that's the way it is. Scientists can explain lots of facts and effects of gravity and know why the earth attracts an apple and why and how it falls, but we do not know why gravity exists. This is one of the great mysteries of life. There are additional forces other than gravity that affect our lives, such an electric and magnetic forces as well as the forces that keep the nucleus of the atom together. We can study them and explain lots of facts and consequences BUT we don't know why they exist. **(van.physics.illinois.edu)**

However, Christians point to Scripture that says:

Colossians 1:17 And he is before all things, and in him all things hold together.

Hebrews 1:3, ... he upholds the universe by the word of his power.

If gravity ceased for one moment, instant chaos surely would result. All heavenly objects, including the earth, moon and stars, would no longer hold together. Everything would immediately disintegrate into small fragments.

Marriage is also part of God's order. Biblical marriage is the fundamental institution of human society, providing offspring for the next generation, an environment of support and safety for the offspring, and a picture of Christ and his bride, the church.

Facts from Familyscholars.org

Marriage increases the likelihood that fathers and mothers have good relationships with their children. Cohabitation is not the same as marriage. Cohabiting couples on average are less committed, less faithful, and more likely to break up than married couples. Growing up outside an intact marriage increases the likelihood that children will themselves divorce or become unwed parents.

In almost every known human society, marriage exists as a way of regulating the reproduction of children, families, and society. Marriage typically fosters better romantic and parental relationships compared to other family forms, such as cohabitation. Individuals who have a firm commitment to marriage as an ideal are more likely to invest themselves in their marriage and to enjoy happier marriages.

Marriage has important biological consequences for adults and children. For instance, marriage appears to reduce men's testosterone levels, and girls who grow up in an intact, married family appear to have a relatively later onset of puberty.

Divorce and unmarried childbearing increase poverty for both children and mothers. Married couples seem to build more wealth on average than singles or cohabiting couples. Marriage reduces poverty and material hardship (for example, missing a meal or failing to pay rent) for disadvantaged women and their children.

African Americans and Latinos benefit economically from marriage. Married men earn more money than do single men with similar education and job histories. Parental divorce (or failure to marry) appears to increase children's risk of dropping out of high school. Parental divorce reduces the likelihood that children will graduate from college and achieve high-status jobs.

Children who live with their own two married parents enjoy better physical health than do children in other family forms. Parental marriage is associated with a sharply lower risk of infant mortality. Marriage is associated with reduced rates of drug and alcohol use for both adults and teens.

Married people, especially married men, have longer life expectancies than do otherwise similar singles. Marriage is associated with better health and lower rates of injury, illness, and disability for both men and women. Marriage seems to be associated with better health among minorities and the poor.

Children whose parents divorce have higher rates of psychological problems like depression and other mental illnesses. Divorce is linked to higher suicide rates. Married mothers have lower rates of depression than do single or cohabiting mothers.

Boys raised in single-parent families are more likely to engage in delinquent and criminal behavior. Married men and women are significantly less likely to be the perpetrators or victims of crime. Married women appear to have a lower risk of experiencing domestic violence than do cohabiting or dating women. A child who is not living with his or her own two married parents is at significantly greater risk for child abuse.

(Familyscholars.org)

Biblical marriage brings order to all human society, so much so that without Biblical marriage human life would not exist. Think of it in light of the popular book and movie, "The Hunger Games."

In Suzanne Collins's book, The Hunger Games, North America has been destroyed and is now run by the powerful Capital and is divided into 12 districts with district 13 being destroyed due to a rebellion. Allow me to digress into this districts idea for a bit to make a point.

What if those districts were ran in light of postmodern ideology where each district had truth as they wanted it to be and no absolute truth existed?

In other words, if one district society in the Hunger Games allowed homosexual intrusion reasoning to dominate and all subjects of the district society were homosexual, just how long would this district society last? If another district society followed liberal teachings that abortion of a baby is fine if the baby cramps your life style, just how long would this district society last? If another district society and its subjects held to the postmodern ideology of the "Occupy Wall Street" thugs, that the government should take money from others so that they would not have to work, and if none of them are working, just how long would this district society last?

The answer to all of these questions, is "not very long." God has setup rules for our society and ordained Biblical Marriage and given orders on how marriage must be followed. Society depends on these orders from God. If society breaks marriage orders, or breaks orders to work for a living, or destroys innocent life that God has created, society will no longer exist. The only reason why we still have a society in this nation comes from the grace of God and people that follow God's mandates. God haters depend on God followers.

Which leads us back to Romans 13. God not only ordered creation and marriage, but also civil government. I believe this is main point of Paul's proposition.

For human society to exist, we must not only have Biblical marriage but civil government.

PAUL'S PROPOSITION AGAIN IS:

Let everyone be subject to the governing authorities, for there is no authority except that which God has established. The authorities that exist have been established by God.

The believer has more than just one mandate that demands responsibility. Christians are in the family of God and are commissioned to share the gospel to the world in the Evangelical Mandate. Christians are also given a Culture Mandate as they enter earthly families with responsibilities to follow the order of Biblical Marriage. They are to raise their children in the fear of God, love their spouse as Christ love the church and submit to authority of order within the family and thereby providing an evolvement for the Evangelical Mandate to take effect on their family.

Christians also, are to carry out the Cultural Mandate in the civic society, with responsibilities within the state in order to live in a more peaceable society of the Evangelical Mandate.

In Romans 13 Paul shows that God is the one that has set up the civil governments and commands that everyone of us submit to government authorities, "for there is no authority except that which God has established."

We must remember, that Paul is writing to Christians who lived under Pagan Roman rule. He is telling us that no matter what form of government we live under, that it is better than anarchy. Anarchy is chaos and disorder while God is order. Therefore, any government order is better for society than anarchy.

PAUL'S ARGUMENT - VERSES 2-5

There are two reasons Paul gives for his proposition. First, God has ordained government authority. Remember, Jesus told the rulers around him that they had no authority unless it was given from above.

Second, Paul'a proposition is that governments are set up by God to reward good and punish evil. This is generally true of all governments regardless of their type. They are set up to encourage good and discourage evil.

This however is not always true. Some leaders become wicked and oppressive which will damage the society. The same can be said of fathers in a family. Society has to run on the principle that order is good, so that everyone in the state lives by a conscience to try to do what is right.

Paul writes in verse 5, that if Christians are obedient to the law of the land they can expect to escape punishment, and will have a clear conscience.

PAUL'S MAIN MEANING OF THE PHRASE:
"being subject to"- verses 6-7

After Paul's argument he resumes his proposition, by expanding what he means by the word "submitting." This point I believe is easy to see.

> 6 For because of this you also pay taxes, for the authorities are ministers of God, attending to this very thing. 7 Pay to all what is owed to them: taxes to whom taxes are owed, revenue to whom revenue is owed, respect to whom respect is owed, honor to whom honor is owed.

Paul's says:
Pay your Taxes
Pay what you owe to the state and others.
Give respect to those that need to respect.
Honor all that you should honor.

Notice that this is the same mandate given by Jesus:
> "Give to Caesar what is Caesar's (what has his image on it), but give to God what is God's."

Just what is created in God's image? The answer is you! You dear reader are in the image of God. Paul and Jesus are saying, give your tax money to Caesar but give your life to God.

The key is context. Does the context allow this last view of the text? I believe it does.

In Romans 12 Paul begins with instructions for the church and how they should live in the culture that God has placed them. Chapter 12 gives 20 instructions for the believers to use in church and in relationships to others within the church and outside the church, or culture

1) Do not think highly of one's self
2) Understand that believers have different functions
3) Use one's God given gifts
4) Have pure love
5) Hate evil
6) Hold fast to good
7) Love each other
8) Don't be lazy, but be fervent
9) Serve the Lord
10) Be joyful with hope
11) Be patient when rough times come
12) Give to the church and members of the church
13) Show hospitality
14) Bless people that do evil toward you
15) Live in peace with each other
16) Cry with others when they cry

17) Do not have a vindictive spirit
18) Feed your enemy
19) Give drink to your enemy when they are thirsty
20) Bottom line: Don't be evil, always do right

Notice that the Great Commission is not included in this list. This is because Paul is setting the cultural environment which allows the Great Commission to best function.

This is followed with Romans 13 and the Cultural Mandate toward civil government. This, I believe, shows that this view is the right way to see Romans 13.

PART 2

Todays issues

7) ABORTION

Some have argued in recent years that the Bible has nothing to say about abortion. The whole reasoning behind this is based on the word "abortion" missing from Scripture. While it is true the word is not found in the Bible, the argument is easy to overcome by showing that the Bible understands that the unborn is a human being, which goes against the argument made by pro-abortionist.

Personhood in the Bible

The Hebrew word used in the Old Testament to refer to the unborn is yeled, a word that *"generally indicates young children, but may refer to teens or even young adults." (Expository Dictionary of Bible Words, pp. 156-157)*

The Hebrews did not have or need a separate word for unborn children. They were just like any other children, only younger. In the Bible there are references to born children and unborn children, but there is no such thing as a potential, incipient, or "almost" child.

The book of Job graphically describes the way God created him before he was born.

Job 10:8-12

> 8 Your hands fashioned and made me,
> and now you have destroyed me altogether.
> 9 Remember that you have made me like
> clay; and will you return me to the dust?
> 10 Did you not pour me out like milk
> and curdle me like cheese?
> 11 You clothed me with skin and flesh,
> and knit me together with bones and sinews.
> 12 You have granted me life and steadfast
> love, and your care has preserved my spirit.

Notice that the person in the womb was not a possible person named Job, but it was someone who was Job.

This whole idea that life does not begin until birth is once again a reflection of what we see in Romans 1. Mankind knows the truth, but because they desire to sin more than submit to the truth, they makeup grand scenarios justifying their sin. I understand the feeling that we want to hide from our sin. It's hard to face up to sin, because when we sin, we not only transgress God's law, we also let someone down. We think of our parents, or spouse, or close friends, or pastor and how much they are counting on us to do the right thing. However, this unexpected pregnancy shows that we did not do the right thing. Sadly for many, the hiding of sin becomes the killing of the innocent.

Again, the reason that any of us sin, is because we suppress the truth that God has given us. As a member of the human race that has rejected God, each person is born a sinner. David says,

"Behold, I was brought forth in iniquity, and in sin did my mother conceive me"

Each person has a sin nature from the point of conception. This means that a person is not a thief because he or she stole something, but rather, he or she stole because he or she has a sin nature that sins. Every parent knows this from raising a child. A mother and father never have to teach a child to push or hit his sister. They must be taught not to push or hit their sister, because pushing and hitting their sister is part of the sin nature.

In Romans 9 we read that Jacob was favored over his twin Esau "though not yet born." When Rebekah was pregnant with Jacob and Esau, Scripture says, "The children struggled together within her," (Genesis 23:22). Rebecca know them as "children" before they were born.

In Luke 1:4-44 there are references to the unborn John the Baptist. The word, translated baby, in these verses is the same word used for the already born baby Jesus in Luke 2:12. It is also the same word used in Acts 7:19 for the newborn babies killed by Pharaoh.

To the writers of the New Testament, it did not matter if the child was born or not, it was simply a baby.

ESV STUDY BIBLE AND ABORTION

In the English Standard Study Bible, there is a wonderful section on Biblical Doctrine and Biblical Ethics. Under the heading "The Beginning of Life and abortion we find this:

Extrabiblical Jewish Literature

The noncanonical Jewish wisdom literature further clarifies first-century Judaism's view of abortion. For example, the Sentences of Pseudo-Phocylides 184–186 (c. 50 B.C.–A.D. 50) says that "a woman should not destroy the unborn in her belly, nor after its birth throw it before the dogs and vultures as a prey." Included among those who do evil in the apocalyptic Sibylline Oracles were women who "aborted what they carried in the womb" (2.281–282). Similarly, the apocryphal book 1 Enoch (2nd or 1st century B.C.) declares that an evil angel taught humans how to "smash the embryo in the womb" (69.12). Finally, the first-century Jewish historian Josephus wrote that "the law orders all the offspring to be brought up, and forbids women either to cause abortion or to make away with the fetus" (Against Apion 2.202).

Contrast these injunctions with the barbarism of Roman culture. Cicero (106–43 B.C.) records that according to the Twelve Tables of Roman Law, "deformed infants shall be killed" (De Legibus 3.8). Plutarch (c. a.d. 46–120) spoke of those who he said "offered up their own children, and those who had no children would buy little ones from poor people and cut their throats as if they were so many lambs or young birds; meanwhile the mother stood by without a tear or moan" (Moralia 2.171D).

Early Christian Literature

Against the bleak backdrop of Roman culture, the Hebrew "sanctity of human life" ethic provided the moral framework for early Christian condemnation of abortion and infanticide. For instance, the Didache 2.2 (c. A.D. 85–110) commands, "thou shalt not murder a child by abortion nor kill them when born." Another noncanonical early Christian text, the Letter of Barnabas 19.5 (c. A.D. 130), said: "You shall not abort a child nor, again, commit infanticide." There are numerous other examples of Christian condemnation of both infanticide and abortion. In fact, some biblical scholars have argued that the silence of the NT on abortion per se is due to the fact that it was simply assumed to be beyond the pale of early Christian practice. Nevertheless, Luke (a physician) points to fetal personhood when he observes that the unborn John the Baptist "leaped for joy" in his mother's womb when Elizabeth came into the presence of Mary, who was pregnant with Jesus at the time (Luke 1:44).

More than merely condemning abortion and infanticide, however, early Christians provided alternatives by rescuing and adopting children who were abandoned. For instance, Callistus (d. c. A.D. 223) provided refuge to abandoned children by placing them in Christian homes, and Benignus of Dijon (3rd century) offered nourishment and protection to abandoned children, including some with disabilities caused by unsuccessful abortions.

Conclusion:

Church history is clear, and the Bible is even more clear about this subject. Every child in the womb has been created by God, even if the parent were in the act of sinning when God gave life to the baby. God created all the children from marriages and from rapes. It is God that gives life to every person, and a baby is a person before he or she is born.

Luke says, *"Now they were bringing even infants to him that he might touch them"*.

Then Jesus called the children and said:

> *"Let the children come to me, and do not hinder them, for to such belongs the kingdom of God. Truly, I say to you, whoever does not receive the kingdom of God like a child shall not enter it."*

The biblical view of children is that they are a blessing and a gift from the Lord. Society is treating children more and more like liabilities. We must learn to see them as God does;

> *He executes justice for the fatherless and the widow, and loves the sojourner, ...*

The Christian Church must support those that are pro-life.

8) WHY CHRISTIANS CAN NEVER SUPPORT THE HOMOSEXUAL LIFE-STYLES

If God has established civil government for the good of all people, and God has established order in creation where He alone rests at the top of all authority with every other ruler under Him, then going by Romans 13, those that God places in government leadership positions are handed a mandate from God to judge right from wrong within the laws of that nation, rewarding evil men with proper punishment and allowing others that live within the law, freedom from judgement. Rulers must carryout this mandate without personal tyranny or oppression bringing fear upon those that do good.

Romans 13 does not give rulers absolute power to reign as they wish. There is only one Absolute Ruler. It stands to reason that If oppression comes from government leadership upon those that seek to do Biblical good, the ruler is not following God's mandate for leaders. In other words, if you are afraid for doing Biblical good as shown in Scripture, the government leader is not God's servant and should not be followed, praised, nor supported by means of your vote.

Romans 13:

> Let every person be subject to the governing
> authorities. For there is no authority except from
> God, and those that exist have been instituted
> by God. 2 Therefore whoever resists the
> authorities resists what God has appointed, and
> those who resist will incur judgment. 3 For
> rulers are not a terror to good conduct, but to
> bad. Would you have no fear of the one who is
> in authority? Then do what is good, and you will
> receive his approval, 4 for he is God's servant
> for your good. But if you do wrong, be afraid,
> for he does not bear the sword in vain. For he is
> the servant of God, an avenger who carries out
> God's wrath on the wrongdoer. 5 Therefore one
> must be in subjection, not only to avoid God's
> wrath but also for the sake of conscience. 6 For
> because of this you also pay taxes, for the
> authorities are ministers of God, attending to
> this very thing. 7 Pay to all what is owed to
> them: taxes to whom taxes are owed, revenue
> to whom revenue is owed, respect to whom
> respect is owed, honor to whom honor is owed.

Calvin says,

> Magistrates may hence learn what their
> vocation is, for them not to rule for their own
> interest, but for the public good; nor are they
> endued with unbridled power, but what is
> restricted to the well being of their subjects; in
> short they are responsible to God and to men in
> the exercise of power"

It is with this in mind along with the supremacy of Scripture that the Christian church and it's voters must examine all issues. With Scripture as the axiom, what then are the real issues that Christians must influence in our government?

MARRIAGE

Traditional evangelical doctrine has identified a three-fold mandate given to man at creation.

1) The Sabbath ordinance
2) The Culture Mandate
3) The Marriage ordinance

Therefore the Christian faith has always held that marriage is the fundamental institution of human society. Marriage comes to us from God within the act of creation itself where God brings one man and one woman together handing them the mandate to "be fruitful and multiply."

It should be noted here that any other combination cannot uphold this mandate. A man and another man cannot multiply. A woman and another woman cannot multiply. Homosexuals depend on God's mandate, for their very existence, but deny the mandate because of self-centered lust. In other words, It takes God's mandate to multiply with one man and one woman, in order for those that reject God' mandate in creation in to even exist.

Jesus says that marriage is a union that God has brought together. Christian marriage moves one man and one woman into a oneness union known as husband and wife. Jesus also shows how the Christian faith does not see simply living together and having sex as a marriage.

John 4:18
> *for you have had five husbands, and the one you now have is not your husband*

Marriage is use as a picture of our relationship with Christ.

Eph 5:25-27
> *Husbands, love your wives, as Christ loved the church and gave himself up for her, 26 that he might sanctify her, having cleansed her by the washing of water with the word, 27 so that he might present the church to himself in splendor, without spot or wrinkle or any such thing, that she might be holy and without blemish.*

A subheadline reads:

> *"American churches' opposition to gay rights is out of touch with young people -- and it's costing them believers." By Amanda Marcotte / @ Alternet*

Headlines like the one above seem to run in the media every day. Christians are said to be behind times for their stance against gay marriage. Christians are told they need to "get on board with history." President Obama, who says he is Christian, now says he supports gay marriage, and liberals wonder why other Christians can't support it as well. Obama and the liberal anti-Christian media just "does not get" the Orthodoxical Christian stance on homosexuality.

The word liberal in liberal Christianity implies a willingness to interpret scripture without considering the orthodox doctrines always held to by the church and they even feel at liberty to reject some of the Bible if it does not fit their idea of what Christianity is. We can be reminded that God has no blessing on such arrogant foolishness as churches with Liberal theology keep closing their doors in droves.

In a July 9th 2012 article that ran in the Los Angeles times, writer Charlotte Allen said,

> "The accelerating fragmentation of the strife-torn Episcopal Church USA, in which several parishes and even a few dioceses are opting out of the church, isn't simply about gay bishops, the blessing of same-sex unions or the election of a woman as presiding bishop. It also is about the meltdown of liberal Christianity.
>
> Embraced by the leadership of all the mainline Protestant denominations, as well as large segments of American Catholicism, liberal Christianity has been hailed by its boosters for 40 years as the future of the Christian church.
>
> Instead, as all but a few die-hards now admit, all the mainline churches and movements within churches that have blurred doctrine and softened moral precepts are demographically declining and, in the case of the Episcopal Church, disintegrating." -
>
> **("Liberal Christianity is paying for its sins"/Los Angeles Times - July 09, 2006/Charlotte Allen)**

The only change that Orthodoxical Christianity will see by changing its stance on homosexuality is sure doom and the selling of the church building to become another local theater playhouse.

LIBERALS ARE ALWAYS LOOKING FOR CHANGE

Liberals, whether they are Christians or not, believe that Orthodoxical Christians should change because others in society have "updated" their views. This is seen as a progressive change accepted by the liberals, as humans continue to evolve. To them, old doctrines should be replaced by culture driven doctrines.

Not all change is bad. A need for change should be reviewed by all from time to time. However, this progressive homosexual change is not an option for Bible believers. Orthodoxical Christianity has never held to Gay marriage.

The Orthodoxical Christian faith still holds to the faith "once delivered to the saints" and has no choice in changing its views even if it wanted to. The key word in "once delivered to the saints" is the word "once." There is no new revelation from God that He has changed his mind on the doctrines he gave us from the beginning. There will never be a new word from God to change God's Word. Christian Bible believers did not choose the doctrine in the Bible nor did they word the Bible just as they wanted it. We believe that holy men of God wrote as they were led by the Spirit of Truth just as the Bible tells us.

It is extremely arrogant for liberals to believe that man can just change God given doctrine. Do they believe that God got it wrong the first time? Do they believe God said some things he should not have said?

Liberals have no problem with changing God's holy Word and show a history of being selective in what they want to believe, but Bible believers dare not take such actions.

What liberals refuse to see is that changing the Bible or deleting from the Bible what they no longer like, places man as the god and kicks the God in heaven to the streets. If mankind and not God, has the last word in what to believe is true, he is placing himself as the intellectual antonym of truth. Is this not the problem that happened in the garden that caused mankind to fall into sin? Adam and Eve wanted to be just like God, proclaiming what is good and evil, and so ate the fruit.

The axiom for Bible Believer is the Bible itself. It tells us who God is and what he is like. The Bible also tells us that God views homosexuality as sin. If you, as Christian liberals have done, remove the Bible's miracles, remove its culturally controversial passages, and remove its sins, you are saying that you are ashamed of the God of the Bible. How then can you call yourself Christian when you do not submit to the Bible but simply follow your desires to change God?

The fact is, we are not to change the Bible at any time for any reason. The Bible is to change us. This is what the real Christian faith is. The Bible points out our sins and our need for a savor and Christ is the only one that can save you. Believing the Bible is going beyond saying Jesus is God. It is saying that you believe his holy Word and you desire to repent (change) and follow Him. Christians are followers of Christ.

Obama has decided to support a sin, well documented as a sin, in Scripture. He has decided to join forces with Hollywood and the liberal anti-Christian media and push for the homosexual agenda and reject the clear teaching of the Bible. No Christian that believes the Bible as God's Word should support him.

Amanda Marcotte's article that claims the Christian church is losing out because of its stance on gays, shows she has no idea what Christianity really is. Christians are not to join in on all the sinning going on in our culture, but rather point sinners to the only One that can change their hearts of sin. Jesus can change any sinner so that they no longer desire to sin. The church through the grace in Christ does not "stone" the sinner, but tells how they may have forgiveness if they repent of sin and follow Christ.

According to Pew Research Center May 13, 2011

> *"While the public is divided over same-sex marriage, a majority of Americans (58%) say that homosexuality should be accepted, rather than discouraged, by society."*

By linking the word "rights" with the word "gay," the homosexual advocate tries to make homosexuality as a needed compliance of the society even if it is sin. With this "gay rights" phrase, they shape and control the media conversation making many Christians feel defensive on the subject. On top of this, President Obama who says he is a Christian, supports homosexual marriage also says that Christians are using "worn arguments and old attitudes" in opposing homosexual lifestyle. This only adds more pressure to the believer to give in to their cries.

These arguments are bogus

I wonder if Obama and others know just how much this crazy idea that the church must be progressive in its belief on homosexuality is an uneducated argument. It shows that those that make this claim have fallen for misleading propaganda put forth by those that hope to push the homosexual culture intrusion and also it shows they don't know what they are talking about.

When Christians start believing that supporting homosexual life styles is progressive thinking and that it is the "Christian duty," after all God is love, they not only need to reread their Bible where it says that homosexual behavior is a sin, but take a course in history.

What does history tell us?

After the fall of man, found in Genesis chapter 3, mankind allowed his desires to carry him into many sins. This is what Romans chapter 1 said happened and this is what secular history tells us as well. Homosexuality is just one of those sins listed in Romans chapter one. So if you check history, you will know that this call to accept homosexual behavior is not progressive thinking, but rather digressively falling back into Paganism that the church delivered world cultures from.

The earliest accounts of homosexual behavior is found in ancient Pagan religious practices. At least, it can be said that the Pagans included homosexuality in the worship of various gods along with human sacrifice, cannibalism and headhunting.

One of the early gods of the Assyrians, which later spread into the area known as Canaan, was the goddess Asherah (god of love). Often worship of this goddess included orgies and homosexual practices.

The Pagan god Tammuz was the Phoenician deity identified with Adonis of the Greeks. Spring orgies were associated with the planting season and a bountiful harvest. In at least one culture, his worship included homosexual activities.

All Bible readers should know of Baal from the Bible, an early Pagan Babylonian god. Often the worship of Baal included a pole, or phallic symbol. One phallic pole many have heard of is the May Day phallic pole decorated with streamers to dance around from the pre-Christian pagan days. It's true that most do not know of the link between the May Day pole and the pagan phallic pole, still others do know the link and still use it a symbol of male-worship.

Greek Pagan culture is often promoted as the most accepting of homosexuality. The Greeks went way beyond accepting homosexuality developing an attitude that encouraged and honored public nudity.

Space will not allow this writer to point out all the history of homosexuality before Christianity. One can easily read this on the internet.

So what is the point of bringing this up?

Believers must remember that Christianity delivered Europe from Pagan practices of headhunting, beastiality, human sacrifice, cannibalism, and homosexuality as they brought the gospel to the Pagans. As Christianity spread through each nation it entered, it brought the truths of Scripture and showed that Pagans were in sin to the only true God. The early missionaries offered proof that their Jesus was a REAL God by pointing to the resurrection from the dead by Jesus. Many new believers changed their life of Paganism, to follow a living Christ that had given mankind a book to follow. When Christians came to power, across the nations, they wrote new laws that did not allow these self-destructive Pagan activities.

However, Europe was not the only place Christianity ended the death centered self-destructive culture of Paganism. As missionaries were sent out to the North America, South America, and the many islands, they found Pagan practices of some form there too. Christianity ended those practices by delivering them from the death centered Paganism and introducing them to Jesus Christ who gives new life.

Sadly, Paganism is making a come back in many ways, with earth worshipping, and homosexual intrusion. Clearly it's followers do not know that death is at the center of Paganism. Today's Christians must not be fooled by the words used by the Pagans. Christians must stand for Biblical truth as did our church forefathers.

To be fair, today's homosexuals do not practice human sacrifice, nor are they headhunters. But they are Pagan and when morals can be set by tribal groups as Pagan practice allows, then it is fair to ask: "What will be next?" Will it be rights for those that practice sex with young boys? If so, how can we justify stopping them?

Moral truth comes from the moral God of the Bible. No other person has the right to set moral law.

Truth does not change.

Culture driven laws are often wrong. The Nazis were wrong, and Nazi ideology stemmed from a Germany man and the German people he led. There was a widespread belief that the Jews played a key role in the problems in Germany. Nazis were culture driven. Slavery was always wrong, but at one time this nation's culture said it was fine. Headhunting is always wrong, but some cultures have allowed it.

Now some will want to point to problems within the church and claim we are wrong to say Christianity has the answers. Problems such as priests having sex with young boys, and all the TV evangelist shame that went on a few years ago.

The difference is that most all Christians believe these sinners in the church were wrong as well. You see, the church is not the truth, therefore from time to time the church will sin. Scripture is the truth. Scripture will not change and it is what we all must follow including TV evangelists.

Supporting homosexual intrusion is not only a sin, it forces our culture back 2000 years to the uncivilized Pagans.

9) WHY A CHRISTIAN, CAN AND SHOULD VOTE FOR A MORMON IN 2012

Let's be very clear about one thing first. Mormonism is a cult. The Christian church has always viewed it as a cult and always will view it as a cult. The Christian church and Mormonism do not mix in their theology, nor can they ever come together to worship as one. This is not even close to the issues that separate Catholics and Protestants. Not in one hundred years, nor a million years will Christianity and Mormonism be the same.

When there is a side by side comparison between Christian doctrine and Mormon doctrine it becomes clear that Mormonism does not agree with the Bible. Many words are the same in Mormonism, so many that talk to Mormons may get the Idea that they are the same faith. However, those words that we both use have other meanings between the two faiths. The sentences found in their scared books sound Biblical because the King James Version of the Bible was used and not the Greek when founder Joseph Smith wrote the books. Biblical sounding words do not make Mormons Christian.

A LOOK AT SOME DOCTRINES

To the Christian, God has always been God.
To the Mormon, God was once a man.

> *"God himself was once as we are now, and is an exalted man, and sits enthroned in yonder heavens!!! . . . We have imagined that God was God from all eternity. I will refute that idea and take away the veil, so that you may see,"*
> **(Teachings of the Prophet Joseph Smith, p. 345).**

To the Christian, God is a spirit.
To the Mormon, God the Father has a body.

> *"The Father has a body of flesh and bones as tangible as man's,"*
> **(Doctrine and Covenants 130:22; Compare with Alma 18:26-27; 22:9-10)**

To the Christian, God is the Triune God, wholly One that exists simultaneous as Three: Father, Son And Holy Spirit.
To the Mormon, the trinity is three separate Gods.

> *"That these three are separate individuals, physically distinct from each other, is demonstrated by the accepted records of divine dealings with man,"*
> **(Articles of Faith, by James Talmage, p. 35)**

To the Christian, Jesus is the Only Begotten Son of God eternal. Jesus has two natures that are 100% God on one hand and 100% man on the other, with both existing simultaneously.

To the Mormon, Jesus is the literal spirit-brother of Lucifer, a creation.
(Gospel Through the Ages, p. 15)

It should be clear by viewing these doctrines side by side that if the goal of the church in voting for civil leaders, was to obey the Evangelist Mandate, then there is no way any Christian could vote for a Mormon. As I have already shown, we are not voting in order to evangelize, but rather we are following the Culture Mandate that provides a peaceful culture for the church. This peaceful culture will allow open evangelism.

As far as I'm concerned, the Christian voter does not have the ideal candidate to support. However, when is the last time the church has had the ideal candidate? Moreover it should be asked, will we ever have the perfect Christian candidate? I don't think so, because no leader matches the One we all long for, Jesus Christ.

I would love to have the choice of a good leader that also is a Christian as I vote in this election. There were a few running that I felt would have made good Christians in the White House, but they are no longer in the race. A few of them have fallen, only because the media asked them if Mormonism is a cult and they didn't know how to answer this. Maybe the next time, it would be a good idea for these Christians that run for office to have a conservative Bible believing theologian on staff to help them answer such questions.

This campaign was rather pitiful in showing presidential candidates, who claim Christianity as their faith, stumble over this subject when they were asked if Mormonism is a cult. It would seem like they have followed the postmodern ideology and allowed it to affect their thinking.

Postmodern teachings say that it is wrong to point out that others are wrong in what they believe when it comes to faith. One needs to be "politically correct" and believe in the contradiction that all faiths are right. That is not only contradictory but down right stupid. Christianity is and has always been, and will always be, exclusive. If Mormonism teaches different doctrines than Christianity, then they are a cult.

Historically, the word "CULT" simply meant a group that had their own rituals that they practiced. In that sense, anyone that worships anything or any god, is a cultist or in Latin, "cultus." This would include Atheists as well as Christians.

Later in the Christian faith, the word cult meant those that hold to other doctrines contrary to your own. Protestants, then, were a cult of the Roman Catholic Church. To this day the Roman Catholic Church calls Martin Luther a heretic. A Heretic becomes a cult when he has followers that believe what he is teaching. I'm a Calvinist, and therefore a cultist in the eyes of the Roman Catholic Church, who does not hold to Calvinism.

I can live with this cult label that the Roman Catholic Church gives me. Why? Because what I teach and believe is not the same as the Roman Catholic Church. If it was the same, I would be Roman Catholic.

Therefore when Mormonism adds new doctrines that the church has never held before, and they have sacred books other than the one Bible that Christians believe, and they have a "leader" (Joseph Smith) that bases all his teaching upon that book, then they are a cult. Mormonism is a cult of Christianity in every way. Mormons should admit this or drop Mormonism doctrine and become Christians.

This does not mean that Mormons are going to drink poisoned kool-aid and kill each other. When people hear the word cult today, they think of groups that kill each other and/or act abnormal and bizarre. However, this is really not what the word means. Again, it simply means a group that teaches another set of doctrines.

THE ISSUES AND VOTING FOR A MORMON

So how can a Christian vote for a Mormon? There are a number of reasons we should vote for Romney who is a Mormon.

First, there is good reason to support Romney from a position that the Protestant Christian Church has always held. That position is what has become known as "separation between church and state," but it's best stated in the First Amendment of the Constitution.

The First Amendment of the Constitution has been worded "separation of church and state" but this is simply a slanted interpretation of the First Amendment that our forefathers never intended the amendment to mean. The phrase "separation of church and state" actually is not even in the Constitution. The First Amendment to the Constitution states:

> "Congress shall make no law respecting an establishment of religion, or prohibiting the free exercise thereof."

Notice what is restricted here. It's not the church being restricted, but the government. This statement prevents the government from establishing a national church that forces people how to worship. However, it does not prohibit God from being acknowledged in schools and government buildings. If anything, it prohibits the government from stopping people from displaying their faith on government owned real estate. Government should not in anyway interfere with religion and religious freedom

MORMONISM AND THE FIRST AMENDMENT

Romney will not move the Mormon church into the White House. The "separation of church and state" is what the Atheists try to always enact when an out spoken person of faith runs for office. This election they are using it against Christians, hoping that Christians will not vote for a Mormon. However, I know of no time that atheists claimed separation of church and state against Obama, and he says he is a Christian. This alone should tell us something.

Most of our presidents have been men of faith. None of them set up church in the White House. Being a person of faith does not mean you are irrational, despite what Richard Dawkins claims. In fact I would argue that Christianity is the most relational worldview.

The fact is, the Evangelical Christian does not want a church ran state just as much as the atheist does not want it. What the church does want is to be allowed to worship as they desire. The majority of Americans (76% to 80%) identify themselves as Protestants or Catholics. President Obama attacks 75% of the nation time after time trying his best to force them to believe in Pagan based beliefs.

JOBS

Many look at jobs as the main reason to vote for Romney. While I believe we will have a better chance of getting more jobs under Romney than Obama has shown us, it is not the main reason to vote for the man. The Church has gone through far worse times than what we face now, and although no one wishes to go through hard times, it is well worth it, if we can get this nation back to a God fearing people. Jobs have to be considered, but should not be the main voting reason.

TYPES OF GOVERNMENT

Types of government will be an issue for most voters this election. Some see us slipping increasingly into Communism, the system that we defeated under President Kennedy through President Reagan. Communism is an Atheist based government that has always failed and has placed its people into poverty. Why anyone would want this is beyond me.

Communism has an ugly history. Secular humanism and Atheist states have shown little or no ethics as their gangster type leaders, Vladimir Lenin, Joseph Stalin, Mao Tse Tung, Fidel Castro, Pol Pot and Robert Mugabe have killed at least 180 million people.

The greatest threat to life in the 20th Century is not crime, or even wars. More people were killed by their own government in peace time than were killed in war time. The 20th Century was the heyday of Communist governments.

Atheist Soviet dictator Joseph Stalin was responsible for killing over 40 million people. Joseph Stalin hated the Christian church and closed down over 48,000 churches, and attempted the liquidation of the entire Christian faith.

Communist dictator Mao Tse Tung launched history's greatest attempt by a single nation to eradicate and destroy Christianity. Mao was responsible for killing about 72 million people, most of them were people of faith.

Communist takeover of Cambodia in 1975 resulted in the death of up to 3 million people which is a third of the total population. Communist regimes in Korea, Vietnam, Laos, Afghanistan, Ethiopia, Angola, Mozambique, Poland, Czechoslovakia, Hungary, Cuba, and Zimbabwe have killed their own people.

Some people want to see this type of government in the United States. The only reason to support Communism, is if you hate Christians. This is why so many Atheists are also Communist.

Support for capitalism, (capitalism is based on Christian theologian John Calvin's writings) makes voting for Romney more attractive than Obama who sides with Communist ideas time and again.

I'm not saying the church cannot survive Communism. After the defeat of Communism the first time around, we saw an underground church with strong believers, both in the Soviet Union and China. As China adopts Capitalism, the church grows with it. Over 300,000 became Christians in China alone last year.

The so called ObamaCare health care law, forces faith based institutions to participate in birth control measures including sterilization, abortion inducing drugs and other practices that are opposed by many people of faith or risk persecution by their own government. This is so close to Communism, that Stalin would rejoice in hearing it. This act is outrageous and a reckless policy against human life and religious freedom. Obama should not be supported by any Evangelical Christian for this reason alone.

Remember, it's not a matter if you believe that birth control is a sin or not. It's a matter of the state trying to force a church that does believe it is a sin, to do it anyway. That is what our founding fathers did not want to happen. This is what Obama wants to happen.

Romney on the other hand, supports the Blunt amendment that allows people of faith to opt out of birth control measures based on religious or moral grounds. Romney believes in a conscience exemption in health care for religious institutions and people of faith. Therefore Romney will get the vote of Evangelical Christians.

MARRIAGE

We have already looked at marriage in detail. This will and rightfully should be a major issue this election for Christian voters. As it was said earlier in this book, the Christian faith has always held that marriage is the fundamental institution of human society. President Obama, who says he is Christian, also says he supports gay marriage. The Orthodoxical Christian stance on homosexuality has never changed and the Bible will not allow this change. Why is it that nearly every month the President says something or does something that causes the atheists to love him and the Christian church to be enraged?

What is Christianity to Obama anyway? Would not a Christian do things that other Christians like? Why would Obama support gay marriage, when Scripture says over and over that it is a sin?

On the other hand Romney says marriage is between one man and one woman. This is the position that is held by all the patriarchs of the Bible, and all the church fathers. The church delivered the Pagan nations from homosexuality. This is why no Evangelical Christian should even consider voting for Obama. Therefore Romney should get the vote of Evangelical Christians.

Homosexuality, abortion, and earth worshipping all come from Pagan beliefs. This is what you see Obama supporting. Christians will vote for Romney, in whom they feel they will have the freedom to worship as a Christian and not be forced to be a Mormon or Pagan.

Therefore again, Romney should get the votes from Evangelical Christians.

ABOUT THE AUTHOR

James Hale is a Christian apologist, writer and teacher of Reformed theology. He lives in West Virginia with his wife Cindy and has three grown daughters. He serves as an elder at Oakridge Bible Church in Charleston, WV where he also teaches church history, apologist and Bible study. James wrote a weekly column that ran in a number of small newspapers for about 5 years, called Mountain Monergism. He now writes as the National Calvinism Examiner

Made in the USA
Charleston, SC
01 September 2012